I0161011

ALONE FOR CHRIST

BY
MARINELA ACHIM

TEACH Services, Inc.
PUBLISHING
www.TEACHServices.com

Copyright © 2012 TEACH Services, Inc.

ISBN-13: 978-1-57258-885-1 (Paperback)

ISBN-13: 978-1-57258-886-8 (ePub)

ISBN-13: 978-1-57258-887-5 (Kindle)

Library of Congress Control Number: 2012945210

Published by

TEACH Services, Inc.

P U B L I S H I N G

www.TEACHServices.com

Dedication

To all who are entering by the narrow gate and are bombarded by troubles designed to break their courage and make them abandon the way that leads to true life. "And my God will meet all your needs according to His glorious riches in Christ Jesus" (Phil. 4:19). I wish this glimpse of my life to be a message of hope to all readers.

Please note: The events presented in the following pages are real. The names used in this book have been changed to protect the people involved. However, the author's name and the names of her family members are accurate.

Table of Contents

Foreword

One day a child asked me: "Why were you born in Romania to those particular parents in that particular place?" I told him that "in God's economy, Romania was the only place in the universe where it was possible for you to be born and your parents alone on this planet could bring you to life with your genetic luggage."

"But," he continued, "with that disease, with the accident, with the award, the school,… what about them?" My response: "They were the only institutions that could teach you what you know now and prepare you for what would follow in your life."

"Oh," he said and started thinking. Then, as if he had been awakened from a dream, he asked me hurriedly: "Oh, and ultimately what's all of this for?" "Taken on its own," I replied, "almost good for nothing, but taken together, all of these elements of your life helped you to utter that 'yes' you gave God that day." Then I saw a little light on his face.

Why was Marinela born in the place where "the Black Sea connected with the sky?" Why her mother and father, brothers and sisters? Why the village roads with mud and darkness? Why the ambitions and success at school? Why disease during the worst time in her life? It seemed chance escaped her just for her to be caught on the last scale of the last wagon of the last train. Why did everything apparently work against her to begin with and later come back in her favor?

She wanted to know who made this grass so green and the sky so blue. "Who made them, Dad?" "God," said her father, without knowing he was teaching her the lesson for which she was born on earth. "Yes," affirmed the mother, "God, made all these things."

The child hid these treasures in the most secret recesses of her soul. Her mother diligently cooked maize porridge and skillfully weaved at the loom. Her father came home with his horses and pushed his daughter in his cart. How could these hard-working people have known that Marinela was staring into their souls and learning from them dedication, perseverance, and courage.

Thus was born her first moment of independence, the first day when she took courage to cast herself into the vortex of the great war between good and evil. Indeed, her parents shaped and influenced her for all of these things, but how could they know that she would internalize them so firmly even to the day their paths were to separate, and that she would stand up against them with all the spiritual charge she had received from them to begin with? Could love received and given from her first family teach her to compromise? No, not at all. There was no price too high when it came to keeping her faith.

King Abdullah II of Jordan writes in his book *Our Last Best Chance: The Pursuit of Peace in a Time of Peril*[1] about how his country's ambassador in London was attacked with a hail of bullets. The car was riddled, and the ambassador was wounded.

"Hurry up to the hospital," he shouted to the driver. The driver sped up the limousine and then came to a halt for a long time. From the floor of the car, the ambassador, who was lying in a pool of blood, cried: "Why are you waiting so long?!" The driver, with his English calmness, said, "Your Excellency, the traffic light is red."[2]

This depicts Marinela and the principle of her life of faith. She has come to know Jesus as the One who said about sin and death, "Do not go there!"

Her great existential questions and many perplexities of life found their end in Jesus. The apostle Peter would say to Marinela and her brothers of faith: "Though you have not seen Him, you love Him; and even

---

1   King Abdullah II of Jordan, *Our Last Best Chance: The Pursuit of Peace in a Time of Peril* (New York: Viking Adult, 2011).
2   This account is paraphrased, not a direct quotation from the book.

though you do not see Him now, you believe in Him and are filled with an inexpressible and glorious joy for you are receiving the goal of your faith, the salvation of your souls" (1 Pet. 1:8).

Her faith and trust in God shine especially when the background of her life is dark. Where was God when she was sick and her sister came to beat her to bring her back to the true faith? or when she was challenged in a court case that seemed lost from the start? when her child was born and her husband refused the role of father? when the enemies lived right in her own home, ready to kill rather than accept her?

Where was the Almighty when justice was trampled and the vulnerable was mocked? Could she say that God was present? Believe it or not, she saw God's hand, especially where you would not have seen it. Speaking about Moses, Hebrews 11:27 says, "he persevered because he saw Him who is invisible."

The aroma of this book is very old, although it is always fresh and spreads quietly into the lives of those who have made Jesus the love of their lives.

Marinela, your writing troubled the waters of my soul and will disturb the souls of many. You did well to have written it. I believe that the same voice from Revelation 1:11, who said, "Write on a scroll what you see," urged you to write this book.

—Pastor Nick Butoi,
Maranatha Seventh-day Adventist Church,
Miami, Florida

Chapter 1

Childhood by the Seaside

I was born in a little Romanian village on the Black Sea. The sea was something great and exciting in my life, its permeating smells hovering and getting lost somewhere high up in the sky. The sun reflected in the breaking wave made the water look like liquid gold splashing onto the shore. It seemed as if the sea had swallowed up the sky, and it took me a while to learn that the distant line where the sea's surface appears to join the sky is the horizon. In my perception, the sea was this vast, undulating plain water teaching me that there are things to which I will never know the beginning or the end.

I lived in a village where everything looked gray because of its unpaved roads and dust, but the beauty of the Black Sea that stretched from the edge of my village surpassed the monotony of it. On sunny days, the sea looked like a beautifully blue expanse that conveyed to me the promise of a better life.

I liked to lie back in the cornfield and look at the sky. The clouds moved like a flock of white sheep driven on the clear sky. When it rained, the clouds gathered over the dark sky like a herd.

Our house was built on a hill surrounded by fields. I used to see the city lights in the valley. I imagined how fascinating life had to be in the city; there was asphalt, water at the turn of a tap, light on the streets, radiators instead of fire in the stove. Later I learned what city life was really like, but until then I grew up dreaming of living in the city.

Alone for Christ

I was curious about who had made the sky, sea, fields, and people swarming all around us.

"Daddy, who made the earth and the grass?"

"God made all things."

Life for my parents was hard, and they had no time to ask questions. Raising children and keeping a household in the village was not easy at that time.

There were four of us children: two boys and two girls. I found out later that I should not have been born; my mother already had four children, and that was the limit for all families set by Communist Party rule. However, one child died, and my father urged my mother to keep her pregnancy, and so I came into the world.

Being the youngest in the family, I would have wanted for my family to spoil me a little bit, but it was not so. My oldest brother took great care to wield his authority over me. When I did not want to eat something, my brother was always ready to give me a reprimand or a slap. My mother used to put the maize porridge on a wooden board and cut it with a thread. I did not like to eat the hot maize porridge; it nauseated me.

"Mommy, could I eat a little piece of bread?"

"Eat that; don't complain. Eat what everyone eats!" my brother shouted.

Even my parents avoided confronting him. He sought every opportunity to punish me and nobody could confront him. My sister and middle brother were also victims of his beatings but not as often as I was. I think he resented me due to an incident that took place when I was on the brink of death. My mother had gone to court to testify as a witness. She thought that it would take only a few hours, but it ended up taking all day long. She had asked my brother to take care of me and provided him with a bottle of milk to give me. I was a few months old, and he was eleven years old at that time. When my mother came back, she saw him playing with the other children. She entered the house with a sense of foreboding. She saw that the bottle of milk was untouched and found me tossing in sweat and blood-curdling cries. My brother was punished, and it probably wasn't the first or last time that he had to look after me.

Chapter 1 Childhood by the Seaside

My sister was very good to me. She protected me from my oldest brother as much as she could. When I recall those memories, I realize God had made her my guardian angel.

All of us children slept in a room that had two beds. My mother stretched woven rugs over the clay floors. We used to make a fire from straw in a stove that warmed, and cooled off, quickly. Later my parents built a wood stove, but they could not afford to make a fire more than once a day because the wood was expensive.

Our family was poor, but this did not bother me because our neighbors and relatives lived just like we did.

I was two and a half years old when I went to the hospital together with my sister and middle brother. The hospital had barred windows, but it was not so bad, especially because there we could eat rice with milk. My sister used to lick the plate because she liked it very much.

"Do not lick the plate because women look at you," I said, ashamed of her gesture.

But she did not take my remark into consideration. I could not help it and ended up like her, licking the remnants off the plate. My father came to the hospital, took my siblings and headed toward the door. I started to run after them, but a nurse caught me. I was the only one who had scarlet fever. I started to cry and shout:

"Daddy, do not leave me. I do not want to stay here! Daddy, do not leave me!"

I stopped crying only when a nurse made me a doll from rags; I slept with the doll in my arms.

I was so happy when I came home. My mother served the soup on a round table with small, wooden stools around it.

"Mommy, in the hospital there is no such delicious soup."

My mother's loom was a constant in my childhood winters. She wove rugs and carpets for our dowry. When she weaved, she used to sing, and I liked to listen to her. However, none of us liked the loom stationed in the middle of our room, not leaving us enough space to pass through.

Alone for Christ

The Romanian village seemed to live in a timeless realm. The villages were submerged in darkness. I remember the smell of the oil lamps, their pale light, and the way we moved from one room to another with lamp in hand. I was so happy when the government introduced electricity to our village. Later, my parents purchased a black-and-white TV. I could see other places, people, animals and plants and understand how great and wonderful the world was.

Water was a challenge for us. A good drinking-water well was far away, and it was hard to carry buckets full of water. I remember my mother pouring hot water into a large wooden tub. She would wash the clothes with homemade soap while I played with the soap bubbles. That big wooden tub served as our bathtub, too.

On rainy days, our feet would get dirty with sticky mud. In the summer, the wind blew the dust over the fences, houses, and trees. Many times, we played by drawing in the dust with sticks. We never grew tired of playing. Mom barely managed to bring us home in the evenings. We would wash our dusty feet quickly in a basin with cold water and then go to bed. The sleep of childhood was so sweet…

My father worked in agriculture, which was collectivized by the communists. He had two horse wagons and used to come home for lunch. I always anticipated his arrival and ran to welcome him. Dad would stop the horses and I would climb into the wagon.

Sometimes Dad went with us to the sea. The horses would speed down the slope. At the end of the steep road, our eyes could see the vast view of the sea. I closed my eyes fearing that the wagon, horses, and everything with it would go into the sea. It always seemed to me that my father waited until the last moment to pull the reins, so that the horses didn't stop until they touched the sand. Then I would feel relieved and run into the cold water of the sea. When we came out of the water, we covered ourselves with sand to get warm; then we would build castles in the sand.

I wondered what was beyond the sea. My father told me there was another country. My dreams and hopes for the future always took shape at the seaside.

Chapter 1   Childhood by the Seaside

My mother worked, but it was seasonal, and we did not have enough money. I always wanted to have a Christmas tree, and only once did have a very small one. I remember running to the tree looking for gifts and being disappointed to find only a few candies, pens and notebooks.

"It's not that much," I said daringly.

"What do you want? Santa's sleigh is empty by the time it reaches our house," my siblings told me.

I did not know they were making fun of me, so I went to my mother.

"Mommy, it's not right. I am a better student than my colleague Monika, and Santa brought her more candies and toys."

"Hey, kid, Santa Claus does not exist; the parents are Santa. Monika's parents have more money than we do," said my mother.

I cried because a childhood dream was broken. I always hoped that there was someone who was generous to offer gifts. An author once said that life has four stages: in the first stage of life, we believe in Santa Claus; in the second stage, we no longer believe; the third stage is when we learn that *we are* Santa Claus; in the fourth, and last, stage of life, we look like Santa Claus.

One day I was at my neighbor's house. She gave me some empty bobbins, one box, and an empty perfume bottle to play with. When the time came for me to go home, I looked regretfully at these objects, knowing I had to leave them behind.

"You can take them home," said my neighbor.

I was happy and anxious to show these items to my sister. But my neighbor friend said, "Your sister is arguing with two neighbors right now. Just go straight home! Do not argue with them because you are not like them."

What does she mean? I wondered. *Am I different?* In any case, I could not resist jumping in to help my sister.

"Why are you arguing?" I asked the girls.

Alone for Christ

They each began stating their cases as if they expected me to mete out justice. Not being like Solomon and not knowing how to act, I foolishly slapped my smaller neighbor. Then I started to run, and my sister followed me while our neighbors chased us. Fortunately, our gate was open and we were able to escape, but I was ashamed imagining my neighbor shaking her head in disappointment. I wondered how much time would pass until we reconciled with my neighbors, because I was longing to play with them once again.

Sometimes I did not have anyone to play with; therefore, I let our lambs out of the pen and they would run freely. I ran and competed with them but never won the race.

I always had one favorite lamb; I would take him into my arms and sit on the hood of straw with a book in hand. My siblings thought it was ridiculous, but I loved to read while my lamb slept in my arms.

I was devastated when my father chose to slaughter my favorite lamb. Dad skinned the lamb and hung him upside down for hours to drain its blood. I tried to avoid that awful sight. At dinner time Mom served us roasted lamb meat. While I ate, the picture of my lamb hanging on that pole tortured me.

Dad went to church every Sunday and taught me the Lord's Prayer. He had a supposedly Christian book with pictures of hell and the dead coming out of their graves, which frightened me. For a long time, I found it confusing to see that book being paired with the holy Book.

My mother was a religious woman, but she did not go to church often; instead, she kept all of the Orthodox traditions. Nonetheless, I felt that God was good to me.

Chapter 2

School, My Life Priority

My sister started school when I was three and a half years old. I learned to read alongside her. Mom was helping her with homework:

"What is the starting letter of the word 'veal'?"

My sister said, "The letter is 'b.' "

I jumped in with the answer:

"I know, Mommy, it's 'v.' "

My sister did not mind and, on the contrary, boasted about her little sister who could read. One day she came home with two classmates who wanted to see me. While I read from their books, they could not stop laughing. It was unusual at that time to see a preschooler who know how to read.

I was a quick learner like my mom. She was a good student but could not continue past fourth grade because her parents did not have money to pay the fees.

My sister, unlike me, had the practical skills. Mom used to teach us the art of sewing, and my sister was a quick learner. I, however, had to keep asking Mom how to thread the needle. Mom would get upset at my lack of practical skills. She used to tell me while cooking:

"Marinela, bring me three threads of parsley, quickly."

Alone for Christ

I felt lost in the garden because I could not distinguish between parsley and lovage.

"Where is the parsley?" I asked.

"Don't you know? It's under the vine."

It took me a while to find it. *What should I pick? Three leaves or three stems with leaves? I better take three stems to avoid coming back.*

"Marinela, did you bring me only three of them?"

"Well, you said three, right?"

"You even don't know how much parsley I use?! Go back and bring me more!"

I was still confused. What did she mean by "more"? I guessed that it simply had to be more than three, so I picked an additional four.

"Come on, child! I should've been done by now."

Mom ended up going into the garden and picking the parsley herself.

I liked to read, but I did not have books. Our village library had few books. When I managed to get a book, I could not stop reading until I reached the end.

"Marinela, get out of the house! We have work to do." I heard Dad shouting outside.

"I'll be right there!"

I used to linger long enough to finish the page, but I would keep looking at the following page.

"Marinela, what did I say?"

I knew I was in trouble and reluctantly stopped reading. At dinner, my father used to say:

"Marinela, bring me a cup of water, and don't be 'lazy' like your siblings."

My father kept on with his "persuasive" tactic, and "the lazy ones" made fun of me. I told my Dad:

Chapter 2   School, My Life Priority

"Daddy, when I grow up, I'll bring you fried chicken every day. Also, I'll buy you a wristwatch."

"Well, kids often say this, but when they grow up, they forget about their parents."

The mud was the nightmare of my childhood. It was hard for me to stay in my dirty rubber boots during school hours—they felt so uncomfortable.

School was very important to me because I knew that only learning well would somehow enable me to leave the village. I finished first grade with the highest marks, earning me the top award. The girl who ranked second said, "My father promised me a bicycle if I get the top award next year."

Our teacher subsequently tried to help her fulfill her dream by giving her the top marks. This was the first time I experienced injustice. In turn, this made me more ambitious to finish second grade with the highest marks.

Although my notion of God was vague, I was certain that He helped me to be the best in school. I used to hide from my family to pray. I often knelt to pray, prostrated myself, and kissed the icon on the wall.

In fifth grade I needed a geography atlas, but my mother could not afford to buy one. My sister devised a plan to get money. She loaded her school bag with quinces instead of books and sold them at school: a large quince for a lew (Romanian currency), a small one for half of lew. I was ashamed when students came to me asking if my sister had more quinces for sale. However, in the end my sister was able to buy the atlas for me.

During one of the winter holidays, I went to school to obtain a gift from the Communist Party: a bag containing sweets and two oranges. I overflowed with joy because that was the first time I had an orange.

Later, a miracle happened and I got more oranges. It was a cold winter when a Greek ship with oranges on board wrecked close to the seashore. The frozen oranges floated to the water's surface. Dad harnessed the horses to the wagon and went to the sea in spite of the terrible cold. He came back with a large basket of oranges. To us it was like heavenly manna.

Alone for Christ

Then another day, my father learned that frozen fish had floated to the seashore. Again he went to the sea and filled a big basket with fish. My parents smoked the fish and hung them from the eaves of the house, so we had food for a long time.

At home I wore the clothes that my sister outgrew. The school uniform was beneficial to a poor child because all the children looked the same in their uniforms.

In the summer holidays, I had to do chores: cleaning, washing dishes, pulling weeds in the garden, and feeding the chickens, ducks, and geese. I went out with our goats to let them graze on and then bring them back at noon for water and shade.

When I finished fifth grade, I went to the agricultural enterprise to dig corn and pick strawberries or beans during the summer holidays. The first day of work seemed so hard, and I thought it would be my last one. But I had a goal: to buy my first wristwatch. When I had earned enough to buy it, I continued to work in order to buy something else. At the end of the summer holidays, my mother purchased me a uniform and school bag with my money. From then on, it became a rule for me to work in order to buy my own school supplies.

Under communist rule, school always started with about a month of agricultural work. Fortunately, I was promoted to supervisor because I was the top student in school. For this same reason, I had the privilege of attending several camps for free, having the opportunity to see mountains, lakes and cities.

At camp we were given cookies at lunchtime; I loved the cookies. Rarely did my mother bake a pie, but when she did, she would put straw in the fire to heat the oven in the evening time, and the sparks—which resembled stars— would float in the air seemingly distributing the wafting smell of the pie.

Sometimes Mom threw some quinces or corn in the embers to bake them.

They tasted so good! At that time, village life seemed so beautiful.

Chapter 3

A Turbulent Adolescence

In my teens, existential questions started to disturb me: Who am I? Why am I who I am? Why do I have this family and not another? I was confused and perplexed, wondering where I had come from and where I was going. Everything seemed so pointless, and I longed for someone to supply my life with meaning. I did not know at that time that "until we see in ourselves the uniqueness of God's touch, we will always want to be someone else and will live under the illusion that being someone else would be better."[1]

One day I felt sick and went to the medical dispensary. The doctor sent me to the hospital because I had hepatitis.

I did not understand why my life took a cruel turn. My biggest concern was not the disease but my absence from school. The high school admission exam was around the corner. The day before the exam a classmate came to see me. My classmate's sister envied my sister because she was not accepted to the same school my sister got accepted to. Her visit caused my mom to panic; my mom thought the girl came to cast a spell on me so I would fail the exam. Therefore, my mom hurried to take me to a witch to undo any possible spells. The witch's ritual scared me; she muttered words while burning mercury above my body.

---

1   Ravi Zacharias, *Recapture the Wonder: Experiencing God's Amazing Promise of Childlike Joy* (Nashville, TN: Integrity Publishers, 2003), p. 125.

Alone for Christ

A troubled soul, I went to the exam, but something deep inside told me not to fear. I passed the exam with an acceptable score.

I began ninth grade by commuting forty kilometers daily. The classes were held in the afternoon, which meant I had to walk home in the dark. I was afraid of the night shadows that surrounded me. There were no houses on the last part of our road, only fields of corn, and I ran until I could barely breathe. Cold shivers went down my spine.

One day I could not find my coat at school. I went to the office and said, "Someone took my coat."

"Because it's not black. The dress code in this school is to wear black sweaters, coats, and shoes," said the teacher.

"I did not know of this rule when my mom purchased my coat. I cannot go home without my coat."

One of my teachers brought my coat from the office. After that, I saw a teacher inspecting students' clothing at the school entrance. My solution was to leave my coat with one of my classmates who lived on campus before entering the school.

When the Union of Communist Youth had elections, my colleagues elected me as a class commander because I had the highest average in grade eight.

Tenth grade began with agricultural work and I was supervisor. I was embarrassed standing with a pen in my hand while my fellow students worked hard picking grapes. With the money earned in agriculture, the high school organized a trip to Bucharest to reward those students who worked the hardest. Each class had to recommend five students. We held a meeting to vote who was worthy of going on this trip.

The head teacher had been favoring a few of her students, and the favorite one happened to be a classmate whose parents were wealthy. I sensed that the teacher wanted that girl, instead of me, to finish with the highest marks.

I did not have a chance to inform our head teacher about the class vote because she had already decided who was going to Bucharest, namely four of her favorite students and a fifth, which happened to be me! I would have loved to see the capital of our country, but realizing the disappointment of my classmates, I said, "Comrade Teacher [the proper communist way of addressing a teacher], we held a meeting and have voted those students who worked the hardest."

The head teacher remained silent for a moment. Quickly regaining her composure, she said, "How dare you say something contrary to my words? Sit down!"

"Comrade Teacher, I speak on behalf of the class. The consensus was in favor of those students who did the hardest work. I don't have to go because I did not work at all."

The last argument was proof to her that I did not seek an advantage. The head teacher could accepted our list of chosen students, but she did not hide her anger. "Because of your attitude of indiscipline, you will get a mark of seven in behavior." The range of grade points was from one (insufficient) to ten (excellent).

That meant farewell to my top award as it was only achievable by getting a grade of ten in behavior! I thought the head teacher would change her mind because a mark of seven was given only to students for too many absences and use of alcohol or tobacco, for instance.

To my surprise, my name remained on the list of students chosen for the Bucharest trip. The school board had added those of us who had worked as supervisors to our voted list of students. At the end of the first quarter, the head teacher said, "You got a mark of nine in behavior."

This meant that achieving the top award was now available to her favorite student. At this pronouncement, I left the classroom because I could not stop crying. I had no one to complain; my parents would have been the first ones to accuse me. In communism, I did not have the liberty to complain to the school board. I was sobbing due to the injustice, and I was sad because my record of top awards was falling apart. The principal, however, happened to be passing in the hallway and asked me, "What happened to you? Why are you crying?" I told her the entire story.

"Go to class," she told me gently.

I hoped that something would happen. My running into the principal that day was not a coincidence. Well, at the end of tenth grade, I *still* received the top award, which meant that someone had changed my mark. I believe God, seeing my happiness, smiled down at me. The following year the head teacher was replaced.

Alone for Christ

The funniest teacher was the accounting teacher. He was about seventy years old. He was short and had wrinkles and a hooked nose. He was hunchbacked as well.

He used to wear additional sleeves over his coat sleeves. He struck me as a very old-fashioned teacher. Accounting was a major component in the school's profile. I wondered why the school board would assign an old teacher to teach a core subject. The teacher was in a bad mood right from the very beginning:

"Guys, if you do not learn well you will remain in the same grade."

After a while, he yelled at us, "You are not cutting it! You will end up at the grocery store!"

Was accounting that much of a challenge? I asked myself. The students who did not pass the accounting exam after ninth grade ended up working as salesclerks.

"You morons are going to sell cucumbers!"

He continued to teach for a minute or so and then made another remark. "You are foolish enough to fall into the pits. You are so stupid!"

We were terrified by his threats. The teacher left the classroom angrier than he arrived. The following hour, things got worse. I met a girl from my village who was in twelfth grade.

"Hey, Marinela, how do you like high school? How do you find teachers?" she asked me.

"I do not like the accounting teacher; he speaks so harshly."

"Who is it?"

"Teacher Loblaw."

"Ha, ha, ha. Loblaw is the most beloved teacher in the school. He is the most entertaining, and he is very responsible. He was a member of accounting committees for many years; that's why he is still teaching. Are you not laughing at his jokes?"

"No. Those are not jokes."

"But this is how he talks, and he expects you to laugh!"

24

Chapter 3   A Turbulent Adolescence

We finally began to understand what was going on with our teacher. We called him "Sir" rather than "Comrade Teacher" because he did not seem to fit in or be part of the communist system.

One day, Teacher Loblaw entered the classroom with a long stick and placed it on the table.

He started dictating. "Write…"

He paused for a second and continued, "From the beginning: colon with a hyphen." (Dictation was used in the elementary school. Students from high school did not need any help to know how to take their own notes.)

We started to laugh, and he began to relax; finally, we had come to our senses.

"Guys, if you don't learn well, you are going to be selling stuff at the grocery store. You will sell onions per liter and cucumbers per meter." The classroom echoed with laughter.

"Just you laugh, but the pig in the barn is dead [one of his idioms]. You are going to sell leeks."

"Really, Sir?"

"Who has just spoken?"

None of us said a word. The teacher jumped up from his chair.

"Where is my *bulamac*?"

We did not understand what he meant by *bulamac*. We quickly figured it out when he grabbed his stick and started to run up and down the aisles of desks as if to pursue the one who dared to speak up. "Who has just spoken? I want to see him." We laughed even louder.

"Guys, if you ever say a word, you are going to feel this *bulamac* on your back."

Teacher Loblaw went back to his chair and continued to teach with "from the beginning: colon with a hyphen."

"You morons will end up at a grocery store!"

"No, Sir, we will be bookkeepers."

"You bet! You will be office mice."

After a while, he said, "Guys, I'll meet you at the grocery store and you will pretend you do not know me."

"No, Sir, not at all."

"Who dared to say something? You vagabond girls."

He once again grabbed the stick and darted in the girls' direction.

"Sir, but why did you call us vagabonds?"

In our class there were only six boys, and they were his favorite students.

"Who has just spoken? Mouse, it was you who talked, wasn't it? You laugh like a mouse."

That became this girl's nickname for the rest of her schooling.

"I do not want to hear from you anymore, you vagabond girls!"

"But Sir, that's too much! Why do you call us vagabonds? Why do you not call the boys vagabonds also?"

"Well, I have two vagabonds at home myself" [referring to his own wife and daughter].

He laughed along with us.

"Take one sheet of paper; I will give you a quiz."

"Sir, but you did not inform us in advance."

"Shut up! If someone dares to copy from the book, I will give him a poor mark."

"Sir, at least a mark of one."

"Zero! Zero, crossed!" Teacher Loblaw yelled.

When his class was about to begin, my classmates were often already waiting for him in the hallway.

"Guys, wait for me in the classroom, otherwise the school board will find out I am late."

Sometimes he started the lecture on a very serious note and we would wait in anticipation for him to say something funny. After a while, he went up to a boy and said to him, "Hey lad, do not marry!"

"Why, Sir?"

"Hey, listen to me, otherwise you will get hurt like me."

He started to laugh together with us. Then he went up to another boy, "Hey lad, have you been to the hairdresser?"

"Yes, Sir, I have."

"Why don't you wear your hair like Kojak?"

At that time, the popular police drama series *Kojak* was on television, starring actor Telly Savalas, who had a shaved head. Another time, Mr. Loblaw decided to pick on a boy who appeared sad.

"Hey lad, why are you sad? Have your oxen from the bicycle drowned?"

"No, Sir."

"Well, then? *La vie en rose* [a French expression meaning "life in pink"].

We laughed, and then he interrupted our laughter with a voice of thunder, "Write!"

Said my colleagues in unison, "From the beginning: colon with a hyphen."

I did not join my colleagues in saying something, but I liked the teacher's sense of humor. One of our classmates had many absences, but she did her best to come to this class for entertainment purposes.

"Have you finally come to school?"

"Yes, Sir, how could I not come to your class?"

"You look like a frog."

Alone for Christ

"Sir, why do you make me out to be a frog?"

"Well, don't you see how ugly you are?"

"I am a beautiful girl," she said.

"Who told you that? Don't you ever look in the mirror?"

"My boyfriend told me that I am beautiful."

"If that guy is not blind, he cannot see out of one eye. Had you and I ever been stranded on an island together, I would never have looked at you!"

"Neither would I look at you," replied the girl.

Teacher Loblaw jumped out of his seat with his *bulamac* in hand, running after the girl and muttering. "You laugh…"

"But the pig in the barn is dead," continued my colleagues.

"Look at you, morons! You come to class for entertainment. A show for free!"

I loved Loblaw because he added fun to my life in a high school that was entrenched in communist rules.

I was seventeen years old when I received my training at a plumbing supplies store located in a very old building. The basement was used for storage space. One day the manager opened the door to the cellar, which was right in the salesclerks' workspace, and warned us to take care because the door was open.

On that day a teacher from my village came to the store to buy a hose. Wanting to give her the best service, I showed her several kinds of hoses. I forgot that the cellar remained open behind me. I bent down to grab one more hose from under the counter. I ended up stepping backward with one foot—into a void—followed by the other foot. The teacher screamed, and then I realized what was happening: I was falling. That very second, I stretched my arms wide, and fortunately, I reached the edge of the cellar and remained suspended with my body hanging. A salesclerk from the basement ran up the stairs, lifted his arms and managed to catch me. The manager came shouting at me, "You fool! You could put me in jail!"

Chapter 3   A Turbulent Adolescence

I cried, not knowing whether it was because of fear or joy. Indeed, the cellar's opening was about as wide as my arms' length, but I could not have remained suspended by my hands given the speed and momentum of my fall. I was aware God had saved me and that I was precious to Him.

On my eighteenth birthday, my schoolmates presented me with a gift, a big doll. No one had ever received such an expensive gift. I learned the secret: one of my schoolmates had contributed a large amount of money. This made such an impression on me that I agreed to be his girlfriend.

My teachers did not like that I was associating with him because he was not as good a student as I was and they thought that my school performance would suffer. On the contrary, our friendship motivated him to get better grades.

I remember my inner struggle not knowing what major to choose as my schooling progressed. I longed for someone to guide me because I did not know what I could do in life. I was aware how important it was for me to make a career choice. One of my girlfriends was already a student at the Faculty of Planning and Economic Cybernetics, one of the faculties with the most difficult admission exam. I did not know at that time that one could ask God for His guidance. I thought my girlfriend was a smart girl and that if she chose that faculty, it meant that she knew what to do. Whether it was a good choice, I was going to find out later.

In the last quarter of twelfth grade, I focused on preparing for the university exam. A nurse came for the tuberculosis test; the only positive result among all the students tested happened to be mine. As a result, I had to go to the tuberculosis hospital.

I did not understand why this was happening to me. I went to the hospital and was sent to a room of eight women who spent their time chatting. I went to the doctor's office. "Doctor, I need your permission to go to school to do my final tests and the baccalaureate exam."

"What?" he snapped. "This is a tuberculosis hospital. I am not interested in your exams. I will not let you go to contaminate others."

My heart broke. My illness was not contagious because the sputum test had already come out negative. My doctor simply did not want to give me his permission. I could not expect my parents to talk to the doctor because he would ignore them as humble people.

Alone for Christ

I started to cry feeling as if the entire foundation I had built during my school years would be lost. Right then, the hospital director was passing by. Someone said, "Coincidences are miracles in which God wishes to remain anonymous." The French writer Sebastien Roch Nicolas Chamfort said, "Chance is the nickname for Providence."

I talked to the director. The next day she transferred me to her department. She had very few patients who stayed in two-bed rooms. I was fortunate to be given a room shared with a woman engineer who kept quiet so that I could study.

I realized my hospitalization was becoming a rather good thing for me. I did not have to commute daily anymore or learn for other subjects; I could focus on the baccalaureate exam (required to graduate high school) and admission exam to the university.

The tuberculosis treatment I was given was very hard on me, especially the pills I was taking twice a week. My vision was blurred, and I was irritable and sleepy. However, I wanted to appear healthy and did not complain about the side effects lest the director prevent me from going to exams.

I completed the baccalaureate exam with a high score, and my hospital roommate was proud of me and praised me to the director.

One day I received an unusual visit from my boyfriend's mother along with the former head teacher who had given me a mark of nine for behavior. I did not know they were friends. The teacher said, "Your boyfriend's mother is very worried. She wants her son to be admitted to a faculty. They know a professor from another town where the boy's chances for admission are higher than in Bucharest. But he wants to go to Bucharest with you. You are more likely to succeed than he is. In Bucharest, there is more competition and his parents don't want to take any risks."

I got it. They wanted me to convince him to go to another town. I thought that if we separated now, this would be the end of our relationship. I remembered the old saying, "Out of sight, out of mind." I noticed some weaknesses in their reasoning.

"I am aware of the prevailing opinion that it is harder to succeed in Bucharest than in any other town. But who knows? It could be that there are more candidates in other towns than in Bucharest. We don't know for sure."

"Yes, but that teacher could help him," said my boyfriend's mother.

"We have learned together and there is no reason for fear of failure," I countered.

"Still, in another town he is more likely to pass the exam," said the former head teacher.

I was ready to give up; the stakes were high and I did not have the right to interfere in their family matters. How easily I could have thought, *No problem, there are other guys out there.* But it seemed awful to me not to fight for this relationship.

"Passing the admission exam is not all there is to it; you have to be able to graduate. If we study in Bucharest together, we can help each other."

Saying this, I had touched on a sensitive point because his marks had increased considerably since we became friends. The former head teacher gave up. My boyfriend's mother, seeing my perseverance, realized I cared about her son and was satisfied with what I said.

Now it was time for a great challenge in my life: the university admission exam. I was nervous about my success as well as my boyfriend's. Despite high emotions, I passed the exam with a very high score. My joy increased that much more at the success of my boyfriend, both of us getting accepted to different faculties at the same university.

Chapter 4

Leaving Home

The time came for me to go to university. That was when I realized why the tuberculosis diagnosis was good for me. I did not know that trials could be hidden blessings. I lived on a campus designated for students with a tuberculosis history, which had better living conditions than regular university accommodations.

In communism, female students had to do military training one day a week. Because of my prior tuberculosis infection, I was exempt, which gave me a weekly day off. My boyfriend had to serve in the army for nine months.

I was nervous at the first session of exams. Each student had to randomly draw an exam question from a collection of questions and then proceed to answer it. None of the students scored higher than eight. I, however, drew my ticket, answered the subject at hand, and scored a ten! The evening before each exam, I took a break from my studies and went to pray in front of a church building. I was always aware that God was the one helping me rank first in my class in each of the four university years. I was given a scholarship that covered my residence fees and meal plan.

I was elected the politico-ideological education coordinator and later became a member of the Communist Party.

After four years of courtship, my boyfriend and I concluded that we can move on to the next stage and get married. My in-laws gave us a third of the money received as gift from our wedding guests, which we then deposited in the bank.

I graduated from my chosen faculty with mixed feelings: sadness on the one hand, hope on the other. The committees in charge of assigning job positions announced to us that there were few jobs available in Bucharest in the research department and were reserved for only the best students. I would have loved to work in the research field, but my husband had no chance at a job in Bucharest. When my turn came, I said, "I give up the research job."

"How come? Think well. You do not have such a chance the second time," said the committee chairman.

Nevertheless, I made my decision: I would put my family before my career. I chose a job as an economist at the Petrochemical Plant located close to my in-laws' house.

I loved my in-laws and sought their approval. I hoped they would love me as they loved their own daughter. Was I too idealistic, or was this possible somewhere in the world?

I started to work, and after a while I thought my whole life was condemned to be routine. I deposited all my earnings in our bank account because I wanted to eventually buy our own apartment. My husband was undecided about this because his parents wanted to live with us to ensure we would take care of them as they aged. Until then, however, I wanted to be on our own. My husband was too attached to his parents, and we could not come to a decision together. Actually, my opinion did not seem to count for my husband. I thought I had a say as to when we would move into our home.

The Communist Party promoted me to the position of politico-ideological education coordinator. I never did like the party's meetings; the irony was, my turn came for me to prepare the politico-ideological presentations. I used the magazine *World* as a source of inspiration. The president of our country at the time, Nicolae Ceausescu, constantly agitated the people with threats of waging nuclear war with the Soviet Union and America. I was consumed by the neurotic fear that we could one day be destroyed at the whim of one person who would push something as simple as a button and thus begin a nuclear war. I presented these concerns as a warning that we had to do something about this. The thought that I could be a victim of some irresponsible, impulsive person who could press that fatal button at any time terrified me. I was looking for certainty, but I did not know where I could find it. I wanted to feel safe, but who could give me any assurance?

Alone for Christ

I did not like what I was doing at work. My colleagues used to gossip and that bothered me. They used to flatter the supervisor in order to get promoted, and their servility disgusted me. I would come home tired after a long commute, and my life was dull. My husband had to work out of town during the week and came home for the weekends.

We used to spend weekends with a family of friends. Rarely did we go to a theater or movie. Then I asked myself, *is this life, really?* I came to a point where I no longer believed that life was worth living or that another breath was worth drawing.

I had succeeded in completing a bachelor's degree, obtaining a good job, living in town, and still, I did not feel fulfilled. "A lot of people, after acquiring what they think they want in life, then find that this 'heart's desire' fails to deliver the gratification promised."[1]

After achieving what I aimed in life, I was still at the stage of searching, trying to find something to satisfy the hunger of my soul. I felt stressed, pressured, out of control, and fearful. We used to work six days a week, but on several occasions, we worked without a weekly break by decree of the Party. I was tired and realized for the first time how important a weekly break was.

One day, Comrade Nicolae Ceausescu, the Romanian president, visited our plant. The directors were scared should the president find something he disapproved of. The presidential helicopter landed on the platform of our plant, and the president began to descend. The people began to chant, "Ceausescu and the people! Ceausescu and the Party!" I did not chant or wave my hands; I did not like to flatter anyone, and I could not simulate what I did not feel. When the president passed the spot where I was standing, I froze as he looked directly at me. His eyes, scanning the group and having detected who among us had failed to salute, stopped at me. I could regain my breath only once he moved on.

My existence was consumed by the handicap of striving for futile dreams, which drowned in an ocean of empty feelings. I was spinning in a circle, and everything under the sun—my job, my plans—had no meaning, finality, or meaningful purpose. I felt trapped in a system that was suffocating me, and the spirit of rebellion began to stir inside of me. This led me to develop an insubordinate attitude toward the supervisor when he asked me to work more than others did. As a result, my work relationship with him started to suffer.

1   Tony Campolo, *Who Switched the Price Tags?* (Dallas, TX: Word Publishing, 1986), p. 12.

One day, we were asked by the CEO to dig up the grass around the plant yard. As they never provided us with any notice and I was wearing a hat and heels on that day. The general director and the economic director, wearing hard hats, inspected our work. The rule to wear hard hat applied to engineers working in the plant's factories, not to the office staff.

The general director noticed me and said, "Wear a hard hat, not a hat!"

"Each has his own helmet," I replied.

The economic director burst into laughter, but he immediately repressed it. No one dared to oppose the general director. I could be in trouble. My sarcasm was an outburst of the discontent welling up in my soul.

I felt that something was missing but did not know why. What could I do to fill this void in my soul? I thought about returning to school because there I was happier, having a goal to work toward. It was more engaging to invest in reaching some goal, but after hitting that target, I felt as if my soul was a desert. I got what I wanted and I had nowhere to continue onward. Oscar Wilde wrote, "In the world there are only two tragedies: one is that you do not get what you want and the second is that you got what you wanted."

I used to think that the things I dreamt of were so important that they would give meaning to my life. Alas, what an abyss engulfed my soul! How vain my life seemed. Back then, I would have agreed with Lord Beaconsfield, Benjamin Disraeli, former prime minister of England, who said, "Youth is a mistake, manhood a struggle, and old age a regret."[2]

I was troubled by a nagging hunger or longing for something I could not identify. I thought enrolling in a doctorate program would be a challenge for me and would bring me satisfaction; however, my husband disagreed, and I felt like a caged bird. I wanted to live in our own house, but we did not have enough money, and I kept asking my husband to borrow the balance from his uncle. Finally, we were able to purchase an apartment. Unfortunately, even back then the Romanian Communist Party had already issued a decree to block any sales of apartments, shutting the door right in front of me.

---

2   Ravi Zacharias, *Recapture the Wonder: Experiencing God's Amazing Promise of Childlike Joy* (Nashville, TN: Integrity Publishers, 2003), p. 44.

Alone for Christ

I did not understand why things had to get hard for me and easy for others. I began to pray more. Time passed and nothing changed. We attempted to interfere through people in higher positions, but no one dared to challenge the Communist Party in any way. I found myself prostrating more and more, praying for God to fix the situation. I went to the Orthodox Church and kissed the icons. I thought, *I will not be at peace in my heart until I get the apartment.* Our family friends saw bedroom furniture on sale. It was an opportunity that I did not want to miss. I told this to my husband and he, as usual, went to his parents for advice. My in-laws were opposed to the idea; this was a serious signal to them that one day soon we would move into our own home.

I was sick and tired of my opinion not mattering at all. For the first time I took the initiative and told my husband, "I will buy this furniture in installments from my salary and use my parents' wedding money as a down payment. I know they had wanted to buy furniture as a dowry."

He reluctantly agreed with the purchase. My desire to buy the apartment became an obsession. Somehow I thought my crisis would stop once I started a new life in my house. Each day I hoped for good news regarding the apartment.

However, beyond the daily routines of my life, beyond all of my ambitions, whether higher or lower, God was working to prepare me for true life.

Chapter 5

I Choose
My Religion

One day I met a family under ordinary circumstances. It was a summer day and I was returning from work. Someone was greeting me at the bus stop; it was a family with two children.

"You work in human resources, right?"

"Yes, that's right."

"We work at the same plant."

They, Gladys and Robert, invited me for a walk. We enjoyed drinking cold juice on that hot day, and then we parted. One day Gladys, looking very concerned, told me she had something to tell me.

"I am very upset because Robert has been attending cult meetings. He has a workmate, Ian, who converted and now belongs to an Adventist cult. They gather together in a house and shut off the lights for sexual orgies."

"How is this possible? Have you ever been there?"

"Yes, I have. I did not go inside; I just looked through the window. They sacrifice infants, too."

"Oh, that's terrible."

"I told Robert not to go there otherwise I will divorce him. He does not want to listen to me."

"You have two kids together."

"I know, that's why I ask you to talk to him. Maybe he will listen to you. We have no relatives in this town."

Poor woman! They seemed to be a happy couple. Never before had I heard the word *Adventist,* and it sounded strange to me. However, I was not the kind of person to blindly swallow any news. I could not believe that the Communist Party would allow this kind of thing to happen. I sought the opportunity to speak with Robert.

"I would like to tell you something," I said to him. "Your wife is very angry with you."

"I know, Madam."

"She told me you are going to a cult's meetings."

"This is not a cult, Madam; this is Seventh-day Adventist Church. Have you ever heard of it?"

"No, I haven't."

"This is a Christian church. I went to their religious services several times and liked them very much. My best friend and colleague, Ian, is Adventist. He has a noble character. I have seen and met other respectable Adventists also."

"Well, your wife said she was there and looked through the window—"

"Nothing of what she said to you is happening. People say these things mockingly. Adventists worship God according to the Bible. Do you believe in God?"

"Yes, I do."

"Do you go to church?"

"Sometimes I do."

"Madam, go to the Adventist church one day and you will see for yourself. I do not know what else to tell you, but I would like to introduce you to Ian."

"Do you know that your wife wants to divorce?"

He shrugged and left. I was very puzzled. Who was right?

Our office's telephone used to disconnect, which disconcerted me. The workers fixed it several times. One day a new employee came. My colleagues whispered to me, "This guy is a convert."

Oh, it was Ian, the Adventist! I observed him to see what he would do.

There was something different about the way he worked, putting aside the heavy filing cabinets and sitting in an uncomfortable position on his knees as if to pray. Yet, since his arrival we never again had any troubles with the telephone.

Shortly after this incident, I was part of an examination committee that reviewed qualifications within the corresponding department. Ian was among the candidates being evaluated. At the end I was surprised to see very neatly written work on a particular submission, which received the maximum score; it belonged to Ian. His professionalism made a lasting impression on me.

I thought about what I heard: Adventist, repentant, cult... People often create myths about something they don't know or understand. I realized that Gladys' statement was not credible, for such an alleged deviation in Robert's behavior did not match Ian's unmistakable integrity.

One day Robert introduced me to Ian, and Ian started to talk about God. I was amazed by his logic in explaining Bible verses.

"Have you ever read the Bible?"

"No. I don't have a Bible."

He sent me a small Bible via Robert—a very expensive gift at the time. I did not know how difficult it was to get a Bible or religious book during communist rule. They were published abroad, and Adventists, not without great sacrifice, managed to bring them in. Some Adventists were caught and put in jail because the books were considered subversive.

I opened the Bible randomly and found the genealogies of the Old Testament. The Hebrew names seemed other-worldly to me. I closed the Bible and concluded it wasn't for me.

One day I shared with Robert my fears about an eventual nuclear war. He said he had some cassette tapes from Ian that would help me. I agreed to listen to them and he lent me tapes containing the book *Project Sunlight* by June Strong, an allegorical story about earth's last days.

Alone for Christ

I had read the Polish book *Quo Vadis* by Henryk Sienkiewicz, which left a strong impression. It described the persecution and martyrdom of early Christians in the Roman Empire during the time of Nero. The Christian faith, for which many people had given their lives, became more precious to me, *but this persecution happened in the past*, I pondered.

Project Sunlight quoted many verses from Revelation stating that endtime believers will face a new wave of persecution. Do I really have to suffer persecution to remain faithful to God? I loved the story, especially the thoughts of a better world. But the parts that discussed the Sabbath shocked me. Didn't all Christians go to church on Sunday? I always knew Sunday to be the seventh day in the Romanian Orthodox calendar. I was perplexed, but I had a deep feeling that those things were true. I sensed God's leading and His call to obedience.

My going to the Orthodox Church was useless because I did not learn anything from the Bible. While listening to *Project Sunlight*, I discovered a different world full of hope and beauty, a world with different values.

After six months of prayer, the sales of apartments were unlocked, and we went to see our apartment. I was so happy and wanted to move in immediately, but my husband objected.

"We have to make improvements to our apartment as do people of high society."

Our apartment turned into a construction site, and I realized the renovations would take some time. Almost daily I went to check in on the progress.

Ian invited me to the church on a Wednesday evening. I could not dare attend his church without his assurance that his wife would come, too. I met them at the bus stop. His wife, Helen, made a good impression on me, and so I stepped into the "House of Prayer"—the writing on the frontispiece of the church building.

It was a great step into the unknown for me. I saw a few people who were participating in a Bible study; one of them gave me the Bible study brochure. I started to read the illustration of the study, "A little girl is sitting on a piano, and her father tells her to throw herself in his arms because he will catch her. The girl threw herself without hesitation, knowing her father loves her and is strong enough to catch her. God is like this father."

I was amazed to discover that I mattered to God. He loved me and I could fully trust Him.

I came home and took the Bible. Searching its contents, I came across the Book of Proverbs. Being fond of words of wisdom, I started to read. To my joy, I discovered some of them that were already familiar to me. Suddenly I became interested in reading the Bible. Unknown to me, however, storm clouds were beginning to gather on the horizon. A crisis loomed just ahead.

When my husband came home, I tried to read him a few passages from the Bible, but he was not interested. Actually he had no spiritual affinities, and I had never seen him pray. It seemed that he did not care that I was reading the Bible.

Helen and Ian invited me to come to church on Saturday. My husband was at a delegation, and I had a Saturday off. I put on my jeans, not wanting to draw the attention of my in-laws. The church was full of neatly dressed people, and I felt embarrassed. The way they greeted each other as "brother" and "sister" also bothered me. But when Pastor Daniels began to preach, I forgot everything. I had never heard even a professor emeritus speak like him. While I was listening, peace was filling my soul, and the thirsting of my heart began to slow down. The worship service impressed me. I felt a warmth there that I had never experienced before. I wished to visit the church again and learn more about this religion that people were ridiculing. I was connected to heaven. For the first time, happiness flooded my whole being.

I went to visit Helen and Ian because I had so many questions. I wanted to get a confirmation that what I was hearing on the *Project Sunlight* cassette was written in the Bible. They showed me some other things as well, for example, Leviticus 11 regarding clean and unclean meat. I loved to eat pork sausages, but I soon found out that pigs were classified among "unclean" animals, so I decided to stop eating pork. I did not drink or smoke, so in this matter I was already Adventist.

I asked why the church members called one another "brother" and "sister," and they explained to me that these terms were taken from the New Testament because the Church is like an extended family.

I could not wait to learn about the day of rest. It was right there in the

Alone for Christ

Ten Commandments:

> Remember the Sabbath day by keeping it holy. Six days you shall labor and do all your work but the seventh day is a Sabbath to the Lord your God. On it you shall not do any work, neither you, nor your son or daughter, nor your manservant or maidservant, nor your animals, nor the alien within your gates. For in six days the Lord made the heavens and the earth, the sea and all that is in them, but he rested on the seventh day. Therefore the Lord blessed the Sabbath day and made it holy. (Exod. 20:8-11).

"But in the calendar the seventh day is Sunday, isn't it?" I asked. They then showed me biblical evidence to the contrary:

> After the Sabbath, at dawn on the first day of the week, Mary Magdalene and the other Mary went to look at the tomb.... The angel said to the women: "Do not be afraid, for I know that you are looking for Jesus, who was crucified. He is not here; he has risen just as he said. Come and see the place where he lay. Then go quickly and tell his disciples: 'He has risen from the dead and is going ahead of you into Galilee. There you will see him.' Now I have told you" (Matt. 28:5-7).

"Sunday is the first day of the week according to the Bible; Christians celebrate Easter, the resurrection of Christ, on Sunday," said Ian.

I was quite ignorant about Christ. They told me Jesus was the Son of God, called the Messiah. God raised the Jewish nation to the rank of chosen people to present the only God and His Law to other nations who worshipped other deities. Jews worshipped the only Creator God. They expected the Messiah to come and deliver them from Roman conquerors. Only a small number of them understood the prophecy that the Messiah had to deliver them from sin. When Jesus came, most of the Jews did not believe He was Messiah and rejected Him. He preached about God's kingdom, healed sick people, exorcised demons, and performed many more miracles. At every turn in His life, Jesus faced threats from the rulers of His day. The Pharisees and the Sadducees trumped up charges against

Him and demanded that Pilate, the Roman governor, crucify Him. Pilate said, "I find no basis for a charge against him" (John 18:38). However, Pilate condemned Him to death. And the Romans were the ones who physically crucified Him on the cross on Friday. After six hours of terrible agony, Jesus died and rested in the tomb on Saturday and resurrected on Sunday, the first day of the week. Amazing story!

"Maybe that's why Sunday became the Sabbath day," I said.

"There is no verse in the Bible to indicate a change in the day of rest. Jesus said, 'Do not think that I have come to abolish the Law or the Prophets; I have not come to abolish them but to fulfill them' " (Matt. 5:17).

I was speechless. They told me Christ ascended to heaven but that He promised to return to take his believers to His heavenly home, where they live forever.

> Do not let your hearts be troubled. Trust in God; trust also in Me. In My Father's house are many rooms; if it were not so, I would have told you. I am going there to prepare a place for you. And if I go and prepare a place for you, I will come back and take you to be with Me that you also may be where I am (John 14:1-3).

For the longest time, I had wanted the saying of Romanian folk story writer Petre Ispirescu to be true, "Youth without old age and life without death." And here Helen and Ian just finished telling me an amazing truth: there *is* eternal life.

"The Bible says that if we believe in God and repent of our sins, He accepts us because of what Jesus did; He died on the cross to pay the penalty for our sins and redeem us from eternal death," Helen explained.

When I heard what Jesus Christ did for me, I had a feeling, an inner tug, to learn more about Him. It was like I was being led toward Christ.

"If the people continue to refuse God's merciful love and grace demonstrated on the cross, they will die and face God's judgment. 'Then I saw a great white throne and Him who seated on it. Earth and sky fled from His presence, and there was no place for them. And I saw the dead, great and small, standing before His throne, and books were opened.

Alone for Christ

Another book was opened, which is the book of life. The dead were judged according to what they had done as recorded in the books' (Rev. 20:11, 12). 'If anyone's name was not found written in the book of life he was thrown into the lake of fire' (Rev. 20:15)," cited Ian.

"Wow! What must I do to get my name written in the book of life?" I asked.

Ian continued to read: "Repent and be baptized, every one of you, in the name of Jesus Christ for the forgiveness of your sins" (Acts 2:38).

I immediately objected. "Baptism? But I was baptized once; I mean, my parents took me to the priest, who baptized me when I was an infant."

Ian then explained to me that one had to be mature enough to make that decision and that according to the Bible, John the Baptist baptized people by immersion. I had heard of John the Baptist, but I did not like the idea of immersion.

"Baptism is done by immersion as a symbol that we die to sin," added Helen. "Our old life is buried, and we rise to a new life in Christ. John the Baptist baptized Jesus in the Jordan River too."

As soon as I learned about baptism in the context of Jesus, my prejudice against baptism disappeared. I went home completely unsettled and disturbed at these teachings. I was at a crossroads: if I accepted the Bible's principles, my life would suffer tremendous changes. These new things cast a shadow on my path. The Sabbath was the biggest problem. How could I keep the Sabbath when everyone worked Saturdays?

My thoughts about the Sabbath went back and forth. Ian worked Sundays in order to take Saturdays off; but, working in shifts, he could do that. I, however, worked in administration from Monday to Saturday. I did not have the option to work on Sundays because the office was closed.

What would happen to me once my boss and co-workers learned I became a religious person? I lived in the midst of atheist communism. *I will lose my job, no doubt*, I thought. And more importantly, what would be the reaction of my husband and his family? I knew my husband and his family would never approve of my joining this church. I feared that continuing my search for spiritual fulfillment there would jeopardize our marriage. What about my family, which was firmly rooted in the Orthodox Church? As far as I knew, I could not hope that they would tolerate such a thing.

44

Only God knew the battle that was raging within my mind. Finally, I made my decision to surrender my life to God and accept Jesus Christ as my Savior. And I was ready to pay whatever price for it.

My state of turmoil did not cease once I made my decision. I read somewhere that the courageous man is not the one who is not afraid of anything but is the one who goes ahead even though he fears.

I sincerely wanted to attend the church services on a regular basis but did not know how to go about it. I kept on reading the Gospels. As I read, I understood that God called me to Him. Anxiety took hold of my soul. The foreboding that my husband and in-laws would not agree caused me great fear.

The struggle of my soul was so intense. I vacillated back and forth, between what I wanted to do and what I knew was the right thing to do. I chose to obey God and go to the Adventist church where I began to know more about God and feel closer to Him. My conscience told me to surrender to God publicly. At the same time, I was afraid that my decision would unleash a storm.

I was tempted to delay my decision until we moved into our apartment; there I would be with only my husband and maybe I could manage to convince him.

I wanted to postpone joining this church especially because I was pregnant with our first child. My husband loved children very much. *After the child is born, my husband will be less inclined to cause trouble in our marriage*, I pondered.

But God impressed me to commit my life to Jesus without delay. I went to church for the third time. Only a few members gathered for Wednesday evening prayer service, and the smaller group made me feel more comfortable. Pastor Daniels was preaching; at the end, he made an appeal for prayer. *This is my time*, I thought. As I felt my heart pounding in my chest, I took the courage and prayed:

"Our Father in heaven, hallowed be your name, your kingdom come, your will be done on earth as it is in heaven. Lord, please help me throw myself in your arms. I thought I'll do it when my life is more secure on this earth. But I learned you love me and you are strong enough to take care of me. Therefore, please take me in your arms and help me to love you with all my heart, with all my soul, with all my mind, and to love my neighbor as myself. Amen."

I saw tears in the eyes of Helen, Ian, and Pastor Daniels. They understood well that I surrendered to God that evening. I was joyful for the rest of the week. The emptiness of my soul that I had felt it for so long was now filled with peace when I surrendered my life to God. As Thomas Aquinas said, "There is a God-shaped void in all of us."

I was not afraid anymore that some irresponsible person could push a button to start a nuclear war because my life was in God's hands. He gave me the inner power to accept and love people. Even living with my in-laws for the rest of my life.

My husband came home for the weekend. I felt the storm was ready to blow from the outside; its dark clouds were moving closer and closer. I was not a courageous person. Many questions troubled my mind. Could I face the storm?

I wanted to break the news to my husband in the wisest way. The church was holding a baptism on Sunday and I asked him to come with me because I was curious to see it. I thought was better for him to make contact with the church. I hoped and prayed he would like it there, too. After that I was going to reveal my decision to him.

He was not pleased with my request but finally agreed, and we went together. When we reached the church entrance, he turned away and left me alone. His action was indicative of the impending storm. I tried to calm myself and focus on the sermon. The Holy Spirit worked powerfully on my heart. With tears in my eyes, I asked God to help me see another baptism and that it would be mine. How would God answer my prayer? You will learn about it later.

I came home and spent the rest of the evening with my husband. He did not mention anything about the church, but our relationship was tense.

I went to work and to my surprise, I learned that my husband had already been there and informed my supervisor that I had joined a dangerous cult. My supervisor warned me, "Stop going there; otherwise I will fire you."

Chapter 5 I Choose My Religion

When I came home, I was up for another surprise: a family council with my husband, my in-laws, and my parents. My husband had brought my parents over with his car for the meeting. All of them were infuriated by the fact that I was going to the Adventist church. My father-in-law asked me:

"What is this I hear about you wanting to become a Seventh-day person and attend the Sabbath cult?" It was more of an accusation than a question.

"I found a church that brings me closer to God. There I learn about true faith in God. I am learning to love people, and from now on, I will love you more and be more helpful to you—"

My father-in-law interrupted me angrily, "Did you forget that your husband is about to be appointed to a high financial position in the Economic Militia (police)? Do you want to ruin his career?"

"Marinela, are you crazy? What are you doing?" My father yelled at me.

"You are so stupid! You have lost your mind. I warned you not to dare change your religion!" my mother said.

As they stood there staring at me, I felt weak and frightened, for I was not a bold person. I prayed that Jesus would give me strength, and immediately, I felt assurance and power.

"I ask you to choose between your faith and living in this house!" My father-in-law demanded.

His words rolled over me like a bulldozer. I realized that my fate depended on the answer I was about to give. Everything I had done so far would be shattered by what I would say the very next moment.

"I will do only what my conscience tells me to do," I said without hesitation.

My father slapped me. I felt my cheek burn with pain. "If you go there, I'll kill you," my father threatened.

One by one they accused me, each becoming bolder than the previous. My husband said that if I went ahead with this folly, he would divorce me and disown the child I was carrying. My parents threatened to disown me and then left. I no longer said a word.

Alone for Christ

"If you want to continue with this religious foolishness, get out of my house!" My father-in-law yelled at me.

I drew back horrified, his words exploding in my mind. In that instant, my world shattered, dissolving into rubble at my feet. I could feel the panic swelling inside. My world had turned upside down. I gathered a few personal possessions in a handbag and walked out the door, leaving behind everyone whom I loved. I chose Jesus.

It was dark outside. As I walked down the road, my mind searched for answers to the questions that pounded it: *Where can I go? What shall I do?* At first, I thought about trying to stay with Helen and Ian, but then I realized that if I did this, my family could accuse me of deserting them.

Desertion could be used against me in a divorce lawsuit.

The only other place of safety I knew of was our apartment. As I entered the desolate apartment, my footsteps echoed through the empty rooms. I watched my step; everywhere were tiles, tools, and debris. I ached with weariness from the battle I had just faced, but there was no place to sit down, no chair, no bed, not even a pile of wood to sit on. Finally, I found a door that had not yet been installed. The newly purchased bathtub was in the living room. I laid the door over the bathtub and made a bed. I had no mattress, no blanket, nothing. But I had God's assurance and Jesus' love. And somehow I slept.

After work the following day, I went to the beach. I laid my towel on the sand and fell asleep—the sand was softer than my "bed." I returned to my apartment at sunset. The following day I received a call from my husband.

"Come home to discuss this, just the two of us," he entreated.

I agreed and headed back home. *Better later than never to have a discussion*, I thought.

"What are you going to do?" he asked when I arrived.

"I want to move into the apartment with you," I replied.

"No, I cannot do that. We did not finish renovating our apartment."

"This is not a problem. I have already moved into our apartment."

"I know that. I went to check in on the progress of the renovations yesterday."

It was good that I had chosen to go to the apartment and not somewhere else. He wouldn't have called me otherwise.

"Please, come with me. We will arrange our apartment fast! We already have our bedroom furniture. I want us to live together," I pleaded.

"And what are you going to do with your religion?"

"So far, all I want is for just the two of us to be together."

"You did not answer my question. You have to forget this religion of yours, Marinela, and be like the other women. If you don't give up your religion, I cannot stay with you, a converted woman."

"My religion helps me to be a better wife. Please give me a chance and move into the apartment with me."

"You have gone too far. I can't take it anymore. I ask you to choose between your religion and me."

"My religion does not exclude you."

"Then I ask you to leave."

He didn't speak another word. I packed a few of my belongings in a bag and headed out the door.

"Wait! I will drive you to the apartment," he insisted.

I did not know he had me fooled; he suddenly turned the steering wheel in the opposite direction, toward my parents' house.

"What are you doing? Why have you deceived me?"

He remained silent, and I did not have anything to add. I could not jump out of the car, and I did not have the habit of making a fuss, but I felt awful knowing I was fooled. Once we arrived, he told my parents, "Marinela has left home and does not want to give up her religion."

My parents went crazy. My father cursed at me and my mother yelled at me.

Alone for Christ

"What did we tell you?" they both screamed at me. My oldest brother and his wife, upon hearing this commotion, came to the scene in a hurry.

"What is going on?" My oldest brother asked with a demanding voice.

"Marinela left home and she is part of a cult, and I cannot live with her anymore."

"Have you left home? Are you going to a cult? Look at me!" My brother yelled at me.

Then he knelt, saying, "Do you see your parents? I swear to God that if you do that to your parents, I kill you and go to jail."

To reinforce what he said, he crossed himself. I had never seen him on his knees—out of all of us, he was the least religious. He was certainly serious in what he said. But I could not recant; God's salvation was more precious to me. I chose to risk my life, sensing that a host of demons were behind my family. I did not know at that moment that God's angels were there to impose limits and to strengthen me. Although they screamed and flooded over me to hit me as if they wanted to devour me, I remained untouched.

"Marinela will remain here with us. We will force repentance out of her through her nose. We will tear her apart by beating her and she will be different in a few days."

Even my husband who had brought me to my parents' as a fear tactic to get a warning from them could not bear the maddening atmosphere. He proceeded to leave. I begged him, "Please do not go! Do not leave me here! Why have you deceived me?"

My cry compelled him to hesitate. I mustered up some courage and said, "Mom and Dad, I have to go. I must be at work tomorrow."

Their hot tempers were calmed by the person I least expected: my brother intercepted my husband and said, "Stop it, all of you! Tomorrow she must go to work."

My mother quickly brought a bottle of "holy water" and sprinkled it on me to chase out the "spirits." Somehow they felt relieved. I fled the scene and went to the car. My brother told my husband, "Well, take her home and she will be fine."

My husband was not convinced. When he finally started the ignition, I could finally breathe freely. On the way back, I said only these words, "You drop me off at the apartment."

He left me in front of the building.

My oldest brother was the person I feared the most. What could I expect from him? He swore that he would kill me. Yet, I resolved that it was better to die with God than to live without him.

I laid back on my "bed." Even though the bed was hard, it was better than a bed in my parents' house. I understood that my parents' zeal came from their conviction that the only true religion was the Orthodox one. My family might have acted as if I were forgotten, but I was right in the crosshairs of God's radar. Jesus said, "Brother will betray brother to death, and a father his child; children will rebel against their parents and have them put to death. All men will hate you because of Me, but he who stands firm to the end will be saved" (Matt. 10:21, 22).

You cannot choose what family you are born into. You cannot choose your DNA. However, you can choose to endure scorn and contempt because of the name of Jesus. Troubled by gloomy thoughts, I finally fell asleep.

After work, I once again went to the beach to lie down on the soft sand and recover the lost sleep. Several days passed that way. But summer was coming to an end. I could not sit on the sand forever.

I did not have money to buy a bed because of my lease for the furniture. I could not afford to buy a stove to cook. On the ground floor of my building was a pizzeria. I purchased a slice of pizza daily.

Then I found a cheaper solution: our plant had a cafeteria and I could afford one hot meal a day.

My husband came to the apartment while I was absent and left me my quilt, blanket, and pillow. I was grateful to him for them. I moved some tile packages into my bedroom, leaning them against the wall. I placed the door over the tiles and the quilt on top, which made for a better bed. I wrapped myself in a blanket and was able to sleep better. From that point on, I did not have to sleep on the beach.

My father visited me at the apartment and brought me some food.

Alone for Christ

"Marinela, come home Sunday. Your mother will bake a pie and your sister will be home, too."

Eventually, I had to face my sister, so I went there. I was so curious as to what her attitude would be; she had always been on my side. But I knew she was not better than anyone else. However, they all controlled their temper. Realizing their threats had not been effective, they wanted to reason with me to change my mind. Also, they were very busy that day; my mother baked the pie and my father and brothers made the brandy.

"Marinela, stop acting crazy and reconcile with your husband."

"I have nothing against him. All I want is to live together in our apartment."

They agreed with that. I did not dare to stay any longer because they started to drink alcohol. They gave me some food, a small electric stove, and a teapot. When I left, I marveled again that I had escaped so easily.

I thought, *At least the situation with my parents is starting to work out.* However, I had no idea that problems were just beginning to brew and that the storm on the horizon.

The following Wednesday evening, I went to the church for prayer meeting. My sister was waiting in front of the church gate and grabbed me when I arrived. She was determined to prevent me from getting into the church building and started screaming at and hitting me.

At that very moment, Ian was arriving at church. He intervened and I ran into the church building. My sister came into the churchyard, waiting for me to come out. After prayer meeting, the deacons switched off the lights and shut the door. I remained inside the church at the deacons' approval. My sister left, thinking I exited through another door. I was afraid my sister would come to the apartment to continue what she had begun. The Nelson family invited me to stay overnight. I enjoyed their comfortable house.

Fall was about to begin, and my apartment was getting colder. During communism, heat was to be turned on in late fall. I got a cold, and my doctor gave me three days' sick leave. I desperately needed to sleep, but my father popped in on my first sick day.

Chapter 5   I Choose My Religion

"Marinela, are you crazy? Are you still going to that church? Your sister found you there. You are insane! I will tie you with ropes and take you to the psychiatric hospital."

Only my pregnancy prevented my father from harming me.

"Dad, please let me sleep."

He continued to grumble and threatened me until the next morning.

I slept for two days and two nights. I woke up only to eat a piece of bread with cheese that my father had brought.

I did not go to work on Saturdays and, one by one, I depleted my vacation days. How long was my supervisor going to allow this? I was the hot topic of everyone's discussion—especially once my husband showed up at my work claiming he was not the father of my child. I had never gotten pregnant in all of our time together up until now, which, according to his reasoning, had meant that he was not able to have children. Therefore, the father of my child, he alleged, must be that Adventist. My husband heaped dishonor on my good name and reputation, which I was so proud to have earned. He spread his wife's "infamy" everywhere.

After work, all of the employees usually headed to the bus stops. I now had such a bad reputation that nobody would walk with me. I could not face their contemptuous looks before, but God strengthened me to walk in His footsteps.

I would get nauseated on the bus due to my pregnancy. I could not eat anything other than tomato salad for weeks. I had only the clothes that I had managed to take from my in-laws' house: a shirt, a sweater, dress pants, and a pair of jeans. I could not afford to buy any additional clothing, so almost every day I had to wear the same outfit.

My colleagues turned away from me. I no longer had any friends. I had no real family. I used to spend my weekends with my friends, but now they no longer bothered to give me a call. "What is going on with you? I heard you belong to a cult. Is that true?" was the general approach. I reached the point of being shattered, broken, hurting, and lonely.

Alone for Christ

> No matter how many or how deep your friendships, however, at some point you begin to realize that human companionship is not enough. Even the best of friends can't be around you all the time. They move away, fade away or die. They don't always understand what you are going through. They aren't always faithful and dependable. In short, if you try to meet all your companionship needs through human beings, you are doomed to perpetual, unfulfilled yearnings.[1]

My world was falling apart. I lost any support I ever had. I left behind my past, my family, and my parents. Many threads tied me to those I loved. Sometimes I doubted myself: *why should I lose everything I worked so hard for?* I did not know that there were things in life that are harder to keep than to acquire. Jim Elliot said, "He is no fool who gives what he cannot keep to gain what he cannot lose."[2] I did not want to lose God. I owed Him all of the blessings of my life.

I was phasing out of my old lifestyle and entering the beginning of a new world that God was opening before me. Everyone I knew rejected me. However, in the church I increasingly became the object of concern and the subject of many prayers. I started to acquire new friends in the church. The Olson family often invited me over for dinner.

I knew for sure that the Securitate (Romanian secret police) would be informed about my religion. The colonel of the Securitate called me for an interview. I felt a cold shiver down my spine. It was very easy for communists to throw a person in prison for holding religious views.

The first enemy of communism, as perceived by the system, was the gospel because it made people free. It was intolerable that a person like me, responsible for political-ideological education, attend the religious services of a church. I had high odds of going to jail because, with my potential to influence other people toward religious convictions, I could easily be perceived as a danger to the atheist-communist system.

I shuddered at the thought of prison. Nevertheless, I could not give up; God was more precious to me than my freedom. I had no money or social

---

1 Bill Hybels, *Too Busy Not to Pray* (Downers Grove, IL: InterVarsity Press, 2008), p. 163.
2 Elisabeth Elliot, *In the Shadow of the Almighty* (New York: Harper and Row, 1958), p. 108.

position or friends who could intervene for me, but I believed that God would take care of me. Someone once said, "Faith is to depend on God when everything else in the world is collapsing around you."

The colonel asked me, "Are you Christian or not?"

"Yes, I am."

He asked me several other questions and informed me I could not belong to the Communist Party anymore. When he dismissed me, I could not believe I had escaped so easy. My Lord was my shield, my defense, and my strength. A few days later, I was expelled from the Communist Party.

My husband dropped by the apartment once again. He found my Bible and little *Steps to Christ* book by Ellen G. White given to me by Ian. He took them away with him. I grieved at the loss of the books but hoped that someday my husband was going to read them. I so wished for that day to come sooner and for our relationship to recover. Later Ian gave me another Bible but could not offer me another book by Ellen G. White.

My sister's attitude toward me hurt me a lot. We had been so close for a long time. But now it seemed to me that our relationship would never be the same. She continuously reproached me: "The whole village mocks me because of you. I have become a laughingstock."

Of course, in a village, everybody knows everyone. I felt totally rejected, like an outcast, as if no one cared.

My supervisor started getting upset because of my Saturday absenteeism. He told me I would lose my job if I continued to refuse to work on Saturdays. He refused to apply my banked vacation time to my weekly absence; therefore, my absences had no legitimate excuse. I would always come to work with my heart trembling, knowing that I could easily be fired that day.

I was in a crossfire, being attacked by my husband, my parents, and my job. I was being subjected to a severe psychological war that exhausted me. I wished to close my eyes and not wake up to this cruel reality. Everyone was against me. Some thoughts tormented me: *What if they are right and I am wrong? Do I choose what is right? Can I bear the consequences?*

Alone for Christ

In those moments of agony, I knelt and prayed. I read the Bible. I could not see the light at the end of the tunnel, but I felt God strengthening me and enabling me to feel His love.

My sister loved me until I disappointed her by choosing another religion. My husband loved me until I threatened his career. But God was committed to loving me no matter what. "I have loved you with an everlasting love; I have drawn you loving-kindness" (Jer. 31:11).

Undergoing the storm of my life was going to prove the strength of my Anchor. When the waves of trouble swept over me, I held on to His hand. However, I was feeling so tired, and God intervened to give me rest. Helen invited me to join them on vacation to the country at her parents'. I had two weeks of vacation time left, so I informed my supervisor that I wanted to take it. He did not say anything and I did not know what was going through his mind; I considered that maybe he was waiting to fire me while I was away.

Also, I realized that my two-week absence could encourage people to gossip even more freely, but I simply could not stand another minute of this agonizing experience. I was already everyone's favorite subject of gossip; there was nothing I could do to improve the situation.

"Oh! Have you heard about Marinela? Let me tell you, she joined a cult. Supposedly, she converted. Her husband claims she got pregnant with an Adventist."

I was an easy target. As someone once said, "Any human jackal makes a meal out of a fallen friend."

I spent two blessed weeks at Helen's parents. They had watermelons in the garden and, having regained my appetite, I ate very well there. For the first time in my life, I went to the Adventist Church without fear; no one in that village knew me.

When the vacation ended, I returned to my cool apartment. My family's harassment resumed. At work my supervisor made it clear he would not tolerate me any longer. Where could I go if I lost my job? Who would hire me with my requirement to have Saturdays off? Most Adventists I had come to know were self-employed and working as craftsmen, thus being able to keep the Sabbath.

Chapter 5   I Choose My Religion

It was late September and the leaves began to fall. I observed the carpet of leaves on the street and thought, *I would even work as a custodian of sorts sweeping leaves off the street, if only to get permission not to work Saturdays*.

My apartment was getting colder and I got sick. The doctor found my lung disease returning. I asked to be referred to a tuberculosis sanitarium located 300 miles (approximately 500 kilometers) from home. I was in desperate need to remove myself from the presence of those who harassed me. I had moments of extreme exhaustion. Usually a person was admitted to the sanitarium once he or she was hospitalized for a time. However, my request was approved. This was a blessing because had I not gotten sick, I surely would have lost my job for refusing to work on the Sabbath.

I went to say goodbye to the Olson Family. An old man, Elder Parker, was there. When he learned that I was going to the sanitarium, he went home and returned as soon as he could. He gave me a considerable amount of money and suggested to buy some warm clothes and boots. He was right; I was wearing a sweater and heels.

I was moved by his generosity; it was equivalent to about a month's earnings. I went to the store and bought a long coat, short boots, pajamas, a robe, and a bag. I had a premonition I was leaving for a long time. Sister Olson gave me some food and books also.

I boarded a train the following day thanking God for making me free.

Inside the train, I avidly read the books and enjoyed Sister Olson's food. She was a very good vegetarian cook.

After changing two trains, I went to a bus stop. The road to the bus went up a hill and down a valley. The bag was too heavy for me. I prayed God to send someone to help me. Then two teenagers came, and I asked them to carry the bag. They took it and left in a hurry. I was not able to follow them closely. It was dark, and I started to worry that teenagers could disappear with my bag. Absolutely everything I owned was in there. When I reached the bus stop, I was relieved to see the teenagers waiting for me.

The sanitarium was my home for the next stage of my life. It had a beautiful landscape—surrounded by forest, clothed in the fall's colors. I went to a room with seven beds. I greeted everybody and went to bed.

Alone for Christ

The next morning I went to the cafeteria for breakfast. After the doctor's visit, I fell asleep. At noon I had lunch and fell asleep once again. After dinner I slept all night. Two weeks passed that way. My roommates wondered how someone could sleep so much. My oversleeping was a symptom of the continual anxiety.

After taking some X-rays, my doctor gave me some medication. She said the treatment was going to affect my pregnancy and that the child, as a result, might be born with malformations; that's why she recommended an abortion. I declined, firmly believing God was able to protect my child.

When my anxiety level dropped, I started to read the first of Sister' Olson's books: *The Desire of Ages* by Ellen G. White, which gave me a revelation of Jesus Christ. I took notes while reading the books and read the Bible to learn the principles of truth, which became the foundational building blocks in my life. Also, I wrote a poem about my conversion story.

The sanitarium proved to be the best refuge for me. I had plenty of food and heat for free. My roommates knew that I was married due to my wedding ring; they were wondering why my husband did not come to visit me.

One day I received a letter from work. I opened it with trembling hands thinking it was the termination of my contract. However, my fears were quickly put to rest; Mrs. Rodney wrote to me saying she was going to take care of my medical leave and asked me to send a letter from the sanitarium. Because I had tuberculosis, I was entitled to receive disability benefits equivalent to 80 percent of my salary. Mrs. Rodney would deposit my monthly disability benefits into my bank account. I could hardly believe it; instead of firing me, the company was paying me. What a surprise God had kept in store for me.

I called the Olson family to tell them the news. They told me there was an Adventist church thirty kilometers away from the sanitarium. My doctor was Jewish, and I dared to ask her for her permission to go to church on Saturday.

She gave me permission, and on Sabbath, I tried to put on my clothes. However, my belly had grown during my stay, and my pants no longer fit me. Not having anything else to wear, I put my coat over my hospital gown and took the bus toward the church. The church members noticed my hospital gown and wanted to know more. At noon, after the service, Sister Flower invited me over for lunch.

Chapter 5 I Choose My Religion

The following Saturday featured a youth program, and I recited my conversion story poem, which evoked tears in many eyes. The third Saturday I was in for a surprise: Sister Flower had tailored a large dress for me; this was to be my outfit until the end of the pregnancy.

Other church members invited me to their homes, and each time I left loaded with fruit, milk, and other foods. They began to visit me at the sanitarium to bring me food. Thus, I was able to skip meals that contained pork. Actually, I made a decision to become vegetarian and offered the meat to my roommates. I received a visit from Pastor Michael and his wife together with another family from my church town. They had travelled by car, something one could not take for granted at that time because one could hardly buy enough fuel under communist rule; the Party assigned a gas quota to each car.

We had wonderful fellowship together. Then Sister Nash from my church also visited me; she had travelled by train, and the route was not well connected. I was moved by these people's devotion. They brought me so much food that I was able to offer some of my vegetarian food to my roommates, who were amazed at how good the vegetarian cooking was.

Each time I saw a car approaching the sanitarium, I wished that it were my husband's. I hoped that he missed me and would someday come to visit me.

Someone came to visit me indeed—my mother. She brought me food made with meat, which, subsequent to her visit, my roommates delightfully appreciated. My mother related my story to my roommates, that I belonged to a cult and left my husband. My mother went to the doctor to ask her to kick me out of the sanitarium and to take me home because I was insane.

My doctor did not submit to my mother's request. From that point on, however, everybody came to know my story, and I once again became the most popular subject to gossip about, this time amongst those at the sanitarium.

As a result, though, one of the nurses learned about me and several times invited me to her house, which was on the sanitarium's grounds. She was Baptist and we spent wonderful moments together praying and talking about God's kingdom.

Alone for Christ

Then my sister visited me. She was full of zeal for a "better" cause. She asked my roommates to identify for her which closet was mine, opened it, and found my religious books. She took them, went to the bathroom, and started to break them. I begged her to stop. But she kept destroying them. I was so frustrated because I had borrowed the books from Sister Olson. I could not stand watching my sister anymore. I yanked the book out of my sister's hand. She started to hit me and, losing her balance, fell into the bathtub. I took all the books and ran to the Baptist nurse's house.

I stayed at the Baptist nurse's house until the time the last scheduled bus usually left the hospital. I hoped that my sister would have boarded that bus, so I left the books I managed to salvage with the Baptist nurse and headed back to my room. I had to return to my room because I could not afford to miss the nightly attendance call. Unfortunately, I found my sister waiting for me. She rallied the support of my roommates, who told her to stay overnight and were looking forward to watching the "show." They gave her the bed of a roommate who had just been discharged. My sister kept yelling and blaming me until my roommates heard enough and told her to be quiet so they could sleep. The following day my sister left. I finally had some peace, but for how long?

I received another piece of mail bearing the court's stamp on the envelope. I was shaking like a reed when I opened the envelope to see a summons for divorce. I started to cry; I had earnestly hoped he would not do that. *What happened to our love? How can he throw away the memory of all the years spent living together?* I thought. How much I had prayed to be with him for the rest of our lives. I did not want for us to separate. I had never been in court. I prayed and God gave me peace in my soul.

The following Sabbath I related all this to Sister Flower. She said she would take me to an Adventist lawyer in Townsville. I requested one day's leave from the sanitarium, and together we went to meet the Samuels Family. The lawyer and his wife gave us a warm welcome. Lawyer Samuels calmed my fears and instructed me to send the certificate of hospitalization to the court in order to postpone the divorce process.

I soon received another letter asking me to make a decision and file a response. Helen informed me about a baptism about to take place at my church and suggested that it would be better for me to get baptized. I took this as a direct invitation from God. Among the books my sister had torn apart was the one containing Adventist doctrinal lessons intended for baptismal candidates. The last lesson that luckily remained intact from that book was the one on the topic of baptism itself. I felt that this was a divine sign that I should get baptized. I began to study the lessons, searching and studying all the biblical references. My teacher was the Holy Spirit, and everything I was learning made sense to me.

It was the end of November when I requested four days' leave from the sanitarium. I left on Thursday by train. Thanks to God's providence, I met Pastor Michael and his wife on that train. They encouraged me in my decision and invited me to visit them the next day.

I went to the apartment, but the key no longer worked. I realized my husband must have changed the locks. I went to the Olson Family, who hosted me kindly. Friday I went to see Pastor Michael, who was the pastor of another Adventist church in the same town. He prepared me for baptism.

Friday evening after the divine service, the board invited me for an examination. The board asked me many questions because they knew I did not receive training in the church's class for baptism. They were satisfied with my understanding of the doctrines.

However, one of the conference directors and Pastor Daniels suggested that it might be better to postpone my baptism. It would be easier for me to undergo court proceedings for divorce if I was not officially an Adventist yet.

A battle started in my mind. This alternative was a tempting one, but I did not like to leave things undone. While I thought about what to do, I heard Elder Parker saying, "This delay is from the devil." Then I said, "I choose to be baptized."

I did not want anyone in my family to know I was in the city. I experienced a wonderful Sabbath. The following day was the baptism. I went to Pastor Michael's church (where the baptism was to take place) with the Olson Family. Thirteen individuals from both churches were ready for the baptism.

When I entered the church sanctuary, someone grabbed me. It was my father. Beside him was my uncle. I froze.

"What are you doing here?" my father demanded.

I barely managed to say, "What are *you* looking for here?"

61

Alone for Christ

I twisted free and ran. Sister Olson ran after me. "My father is here," I told her.

She quickly took me to the room where the women were preparing for baptism and locked the door behind me. She assigned a young, robust, tall Adventist man to guard our door. I found that my mother was here too; she came to the door but was deterred by the stature of the man guard the door. I was further surprised to find that my oldest brother was there too; he was patrolling the churchyard. My father and uncle sat in the back seats and my mom in one of the front seats.

How come all of them are in church? I wondered. Someone must have seen me in church on Sabbath and told my parents that I was in town, probably for the baptism the following day.

Throughout the pastor's sermon and baptism, I remained hidden. One by one the baptismal candidates were immersed in the water. Three pastors were in charge: Pastor Daniels, Pastor Michael, and one of the conference directors. Sister Olson, a former security officer, placed several deacons in front of the baptistry to discourage anyone who would want to prevent or intervene in the baptism. Sister Olson signaled to me, and I made my way from the room to the baptistry. I heard my mother shouting: "Marinela, what are you doing? Don't abandon your parents' religion!"

With my heart trembling, I walked into the water. The pastor lifted his hand over my head and prayed, then quickly dipped me backward into the water. I had a feeling I cannot adequately describe. Having lived near the seashore, I went underwater often but have never experienced this particular feeling. It was sweet and peaceful; it was like being transported into another world for a moment and then returning when the water entered my nose.

My mother left the sanctuary. Now baptized and a *bona fide* church member, I felt warmed by the smile of God. Everything around me seemed somehow more glorious and new.

After changing their wet gowns, all those baptized stepped on the platform. I had enough courage to stand with them. I asked Pastor Michael, "Could I recite a poem?"

He made motioned to me to go take the microphone. I recited my conversion story poem. I recited it with pathos, especially for my father and uncle, who were still in the church sanctuary. I saw tears in people's eyes. I learned that a family who had been putting off their decision to be baptized made their decision right then.

When the church members came to greet us, I received the most bouquets of flowers. I retired with them into the room and reluctantly had to leave them there. In the meantime, Sister Olson investigated the situation outside: my mother and brother were blocking the exits. Sister Olson suggested that I escape through a window. She asked a deacon to remove the window in the room where I was hiding. Sister Olson asked me to jump through the opening. That was more easily said than done given my big, pregnant belly. I crawled out, climbed over a fence into a neighbor's courtyard, and hurried to the street where a car was waiting. I must have looked quite humorous as a pregnant lady clumsily crawling through a window and over a fence, but God helped me. I climbed into the car and lay on the back seat while Sister Olson drove to her apartment, where I'd be safe.

My parents stirred a scandal in the churchyard when they realized I had escaped. Later they filed a complaint at the Department of Religious Affairs, and Pastor Daniels was called to account for the baptism performed.

The next day, Pastor Michael and his wife took me to the sanitarium by car. I realized the biggest attack of the devil was to prevent me from getting baptized. In the great controversy between God and Satan, a person must decide whose side he or she will be on. Baptism gave me an identity: God's child. No one can steal your identity in Christ.

The Samuels family (Adventist attorney) visited me at the sanitarium—right on time; my doctor was about to discharge me from the sanitarium. They spoke with her and their persuasion was so effective that my doctor gave up her plan.

Christmas was approaching when my mother came to visit me again. She brought me pork sausages, which I used to enjoy. She knew I had stopped eating pork, but she likely wanted to tempt me.

Alone for Christ

Mom came with the same complaints, but she did not have the same zeal as before. The dice had been cast. She had to accept I was an Adventist.

The Samuels family invited me to spend the winter holiday with them. We went to church and had a fellowship meal where they invited some young members. While we were singing Christian hymns, a young person played the piano. He had an extraordinary talent. He was a new convert who had given up a promising career that would not allow him to keep the Sabbath.

I returned to the sanitarium and few days later—I had lost blood. The ambulance took me to the maternity ward, which was located in Townsville. Sister Samuels knew a good doctor and asked him to take me in as his patient. After I received my treatment, my pregnancy was out of danger and the doctor proceeded to get me discharged.

Sister Samuels told him that I had nowhere to go. The doctor was moved and delayed the discharge for a while. The maternity rooms became overcrowded, and for a few nights, we all slept two to a bed.

I ask God to work on my behalf and lead my doctor not to discharge me. Every day when my doctor came to my bed, I envisioned that I put my hand in Jesus' hand and that nothing bad could touch me. Later my doctor told Sister Samuels that each time he came to my bed, he was unable to tell me to leave the hospital.

Many church members visited me and brought me so much food that I shared some of it with the other patients.

One day my sister paid me a visit. She was not allowed to enter my room. She stood outside of the room grumbling to me for a while, and then she left.

I was so grateful to God for His provisions. Many pregnant women had to go to work by bus and attend to housework. As for me, someone else placed meals on the table in front of me for six months, and I did not have to go to work. My heavenly Father took good care of me.

I was always afraid of birthing labor. Before my conversion, I remember reading in the newspaper that in Russia they were experimenting with birthing in water to reduce labor pain. I had fantasized that I would have enough money to afford to go to Russia to deliver my child.

However, I was not afraid anymore because I trusted God to assist me during birth. That moment came on Sunday night, when my water broke. The next morning the hospital staff transferred me to the labor section. The labor pains did not come all day long. On Monday night my doctor gave me an injection. The women around me were screaming in pain. Hours passed and I still felt nothing. My doctor came back and hooked me up to an IV. He had a tough night, having performed three caesarean surgeries.

Drop after drop fell slowly from the IV, and my labor pains finally began. One of my roommates came to me; she confessed she was a believer, too. She asked me what name I had chosen for my child.

" 'Emanuel,' if it's a boy, which means 'God with us.' "

She liked the name and I later found out that she gave her son the same name. The labor pains intensified, and I called on Jesus to help me. My roommate called a nurse, who then took me to the delivery room. On the way down, I did not feel any pain. When I got there, I smiled at the two midwives. They said that nobody ever entered the delivery room smiling. It was 1:50 in the morning when they called the doctor. I told him, "Doctor, you must be tired after three cesarean surgeries, and I do not want to cause you any trouble."

My doctor stood by to watch the delivery. I felt incredible strength and not a semblance of pain. After ten minutes, I heard my baby's first cry.

"You have a boy," the doctor said.

I exclaimed, "Exactly, what I wanted!"

My doctor told Sister Samuels he could not believe how confident I was and how I worried for him and not for myself at that moment.

I myself wondered how I could have possibly delivered a child without pain. God worked this miracle for me. My child was born the day before my birthday. The good Lord knows how to give real gifts to His children.

I shared my joy with my sisters from church who visited me. One of them suggested that I use my husband's first name as my child's middle name; this would melt my husband's heart. I thought perhaps this sister was right, and I agreed to give my baby a middle name.

Alone for Christ

I experienced my first challenge the day after delivery when a police officer came to register the children for birth certificates. My child had no father to attest to the child's identity. I had no marriage certificate with me, only my identification. Therefore, I was categorized along with women who had illegitimate children.

I burst into tears. The police officer told me gently that crying affects breastfeeding. I told him about my husband's refusal to claim his child. The Holy Spirit convicted the police officer that I was not a prostitute. Although it was illegal to do so, he recorded my husband's name on the birth certificate. This enabled my son and I to receive child support.

Sister Parson brought me baby clothes and diapers, and I left the hospital with my baby dressed like a prince. Sister Davis took my baby and me to her home. The Davis family gave me the only room that was heated, and they slept in the cold living room. Their sacrifice for a foreigner like me left me speechless.

I received visits from many church members, who brought me a crib, stroller, and clothes for the baby as well as for me. I had never met anyone better than the people from church. When I started going to church again, some of my sisters slipped some money in my pocket.

My husband was very angry when he learned that my child was registered in his name. Forty days postpartum, I was summoned to court regarding the denial of paternity. This had to be the first trial of my life. Helen sent me an inspiring letter with the following Bible verse: "You will not have to fight in this battle. Take up your positions; stand firm and see the deliverance the Lord will give you" (2 Chron. 20:17). This promise gave me courage.

I left my baby with Sister Davis and, accompanied by the Samuels family, went to the trial, which was scheduled to take place in my town. When we arrived, Sister Olson came to me with a woman attorney. I never did find out who had paid to retain an attorney on my behalf. Also present were two other sisters from my church.

I looked around for my family; none of them were there. It was a good thing they had not learned about the trial. I was dressed in the best clothes that I had been given. I purchased a hat with a matching scarf to complete my outfit and look nice.

Chapter 5   I Choose My Religion

My husband came to the courthouse, appearing full of himself, accompanied by his lawyer. When he saw me, he burst into a scornful laugh, but when he saw I had a lawyer, he appeared less confident. The trial began, and, to my surprise, his lawyer stated that her client acknowledged the child. There was no longer a need for any paternity tests. The divine promise was fulfilled precisely: I did not have to fight in this battle. I saw the deliverance of my Lord.

I came back to Townsville. My mother found the address of Family Samuels and went there. I went to meet her alone, without my child. I did not know whether my mother's attitude had changed. I decided that if she wanted to see the child, I would bring her to Family Davis, my host. My mother, however, had no interest in this regard. She accused Family Samuels of abducting me. Then she left. After nearly two months, I moved in with Family Samuels, who gave me their room.

My father and my sister visited me there. They came with the same charges as my mother had. Upon leaving, they went directly to the police, where they complained that I had been abducted by members of a religious cult.

A police officer knocked on the door. He entered the house and saw Sister Samuels washing my baby clothes. He became acquainted with Brother Samuels, the lawyer.

I was in the baby's room dressed in a nice robe, which one of the church members had purchased for me. What most impressed the police officer were the boxes of baby formula by the brand Humana, imported from Germany. He told us that he was rarely able to get this kind of milk for his child and that this favorably testified of the privileges that I enjoyed in that house. He dismissed my family's accusations.

The time for the first divorce hearing came. Again, the Samuels family accompanied me. Sister Olson was there waiting for me with the same lawyer as before. Three other church members were there. I made a statement in court: "I do not want a divorce." My stance was true and biblical.

The time came for my witnesses, Helen and another church member, to testify.

Alone for Christ

Then my husband's witnesses came to the stand: the first one was his cousin, and the second ... well, the second one was my mother. I was shocked. My mother started to accuse me in court, and what an impression her testimony made! However, the process was delayed because I did not want a divorce.

My father was in the courtroom, too. My parents were complaining loudly in the hallway. People intending to see the commotion came closer. I managed to leave, but my parents followed me, and the crowd, too. My parents caught up to me. Brother Samuels wanted to talk to them, but my mother began to yell: "Jump, people! My daughter has joined a cult. These are the members of the cult who want to take her with them!"

More people gathered around us, and some of them started to threaten the Samuels family and other church members. Soon the crowd was wedged between my brethren and me and I could not see them anymore.

The crowd started to shout one thing upon another. A woman spat in my face. I smelled alcohol on her breath. I remembered at that moment how a crowd spat in Jesus' face too. I could hardly manage to say something to cut through all the noise. A woman expressed her mercy toward me, saying, "Leave the woman alone! Why do you immobilize her?"

Immediately she received angry glances and withdrew from the crowd. The pressure on me was overwhelming. The noise of the crowd was getting louder. The scene must have resembled something scandalous. It seemed as if a journalist would come at any moment and I would be on the front page of the newspaper. Even if I had to endure this kind of shame, I would. However, it was not a journalist who came, but a police officer. The crowd was silent and my parents began to protest.

I told the police officer, "I am an adult, I chose to live in another town, where my baby is currently being babysat, and I need to go back to him." The police officer took my identification data and went to his supervisor.

I had not done anything against law, and the police officer ought to have intervened against the crowd that had blocked my way. I think he was afraid to do so, because he did not come back.

It is amazing how God strengthens you. I was not afraid anymore. More people from the courthouse went outside to see what would happen. At one point even my lawyer came. I told her that I was waiting for the police officer.

It was a very hot day, and my lawyer suggested that we go back into the courthouse. My parents had some respect for my lawyer and allowed me to return to the hall. The mob entered behind me, and, in an effort to anchor myself, I gripped a pole.

My parents grew tired of waiting. Dad started to pull me away from the pole but he could not, for I hung on as tightly as I could. I got hungry, so I pulled a biscuit out of my bag. I was holding on to the pole with one hand and eating with the other. Someone said, "Look at her! She is eating...."

They looked at me as if I were a creature from another planet. At one point, I saw my father talking to a man. The next moment both the man and my father rushed toward me, pulled me away with them and pushed me through the exit. Another "kind" man volunteered his vehicle. They pushed me into his car with my parents sitting on both sides of me. My father gave the driver their address.

I thought God had forsaken me. My plan was to live in Townsville. The church members were so kind to me, and I could find some work through them. I did not want to go back to my parents' home only to give them the opportunity to harass me again. I did not know how they were going to treat me. I remembered the words of Jesus: "A man's enemies will be the members of his own household" (Matt. 10:36).

I did not understand why God allowed me to be taken by force. Pastor Sorin Petrof said in a sermon:

> God will always be there with you in any situation you are, even if you do not understand what is happening, even if you do not understand the route, even if you think He forsook you. God does not explain His actions because you cannot understand them. In His plans, you are not alone, just you and your problems, but others are involved too, and He considers them. His plan may seem tortuous and hard to understand, but ultimately, when you draw the line, you will see a perfect harmony. Even though the road was not simple and easy, you will see that the result is perfect. Only God can do in any situation of life an opportunity to go further and to develop your relationship with Him. You have to discover for yourself His power and His presence; He is willing to get involved in every detail of your life, even if you do not perceive it and have the feeling that He is far from you.

Alone for Christ

I was scared but determined to remain faithful no matter what. God strengthened me and once we arrived home, I said, "I will live with you, but I will go to church every Saturday."

They nodded, partly because they were exhausted. The next day I told them that I needed to go to my baby. I promised that I would come back.

I learned what else had happened at the courthouse where the mob had lost all reason. Not only did they drive the church members away, but they pulled thistles with which to hit Sister Samuels. They even tried to push her into a nearby ravine. I told Family Samuels that I had to go back to my parents as I promised. They said it would be better to leave my child in their care until I saw how my family would act. Turn the page, and you will see for yourself.

Chapter 6

Back to the Village

It is very difficult for someone to return to his parents' home out of defeat. People look at you with boundless contempt. One day you are on top of the world; the next, you are an outcast. Yesterday you were an example for the village; today, you are a nobody. Yet, I continued on the rough path of faith trusting my Lord would not abandon me.

I returned to my village with a sorrowful heart. How hard I had worked to leave the countryside. Being back meant having to deal with my oldest brother once again. He no longer lived with my parents, but he lived close enough to be able to come quite often. I had to live with my sister, who was not the same good sister to me.

Living in the village meant treading through the mud again; many years had passed since my childhood, but the roads remained unpaved. Who knew? How much would I have to endure from my parents while living under their roof?

For instance, my mother told me I could not have possibly brought them greater shame even if I had been a whore. All of their accusations hurt me. But I could not doubt one thing: God was with me, and my cause was right before Him.

My maternity leave ended, and it was the time to resume my work. I did not want to go back to the plant where I had been singled out as the black sheep. However, I realized that God's will for me was to be a witness to my faith. At the plant nine months later, I realized the attitude of my colleagues toward me was softer than before.

Alone for Christ

I met with Mrs. Rodney, who handed me a bank statement showing my disability benefits for the past months. Jesus said, "I tell you the truth; whatever you did for one of least of these brothers of mine, you did for me" (Matt. 25:40).

The money deposited in the bank offered me a degree of independence. I could purchase train tickets to go see my child almost every weekend. My clothes were still in my husband's possession, and now I could afford to purchase some.

One of my colleagues said, "You used to be an elegant woman, but not anymore. You have even changed the way you walk."

She was right; God had changed me. Back when I had started to wear a hat, I walked with "my nose up," aware that I looked good. As I strutted I did not notice the edge of the pavement, tripped, and fell down. My hat rolled away on the road. I could not have been more embarrassed. I hurried after my hat; the cars were moving closer. I lifted it up and saw how dirty it was. I walked away with my hat in hand having learned the first lesson in humility. I had many other lessons to learn.

I felt I had changed. Things that had seemed so right and familiar before my conversion were no longer important or valuable to me. My goals, dreams, and desires had changed. When I commuted before my conversion, I used to admire the elegant hotels. After my conversion, the buildings were not attractive anymore and my eyes instead delighted to look at the trees, grass, and especially at the Black Sea. That is because the Holy Spirit was working in me.

I started to appreciate my work, and my supervisor's demands no longer bothered me. I felt that my thinking had shifted 180 degrees. It was as if I was a different person. What a paradox: to be both the same and yet different. My encounter with Christ was definitely the turning point in my life.

> To be converted is to enter into a close personal relationship with the resurrected Jesus. The Christian experiences the world through the eyes of Christ and is in the process of being transformed into someone who thinks like Jesus. This means that people you could not stand prior to conversion, you are capable of loving after conversion. It means that a job that might not have excited you

because it did not pay well or seem prestigious becomes a channel through which you can serve others in the name of Christ.[1]

At work my greatest challenge was to get Saturdays off. However, the administrative staff could opt to work security overnight in exchange for two days off. Not everyone's request was granted. What chance did a Christian have to be able to guard a plant, the bastion of communism? And yet, I found favor with the person responsible for scheduling night shifts on security; I remained on duty one night and then worked the following day in order to be free on Saturdays. I could barely keep my eyes open at work the day after the night shift, but I was happy to be able to keep the Sabbath.

I went to church on Saturday, and my parents did not like it. My mother told me, "Stop going to church! You can keep your faith while staying at home."

In my hostile world where I felt threatened, I turned to the church for fellowship and support. Meeting people who shared the same hope and faith foundation gave me the motivation to keep moving forward. I spiritually grew up in the church; I could not get the teachings from any other place.

Elton Trueblood wrote, "Though I am as conscious as are most people of the inadequacies of the local church and though I am sure that the church is not the building... I can never forget that, apart from the poor little fellowships in such poor buildings, there isn't a chance in the world that I would be enlisted in the cause of Christ."[2]

My parents saw my religion as an affront to theirs, even a threat.

Therefore, they tried to convince me that I was wrong and they were on track. I hid from them whenever I read the Bible. I studied the Sabbath School lessons on the bus on my way to work. It was a relief for me whenever I could leave the house. I volunteered, whenever I could, to go to our headquarters, which was pretty close to Townsville. I arranged to be there on Fridays so I could spend the Sabbath with my child and Family Samuels.

---

1   Tony Campolo, *Who Switched the Price Tags?* (Dallas, TX: Word Publishing, 1986), p. 111.
2   Ravi Zacharias, *Recapture the Wonder: Experiencing God's Amazing Promise of Childlike Joy* (Nashville, TN: Integrity Publishers, 2003), pp. 161, 162.

Alone for Christ

Most weekends, I would leave at night to catch the train. There were still cornfields and dark roads near my parents' home. However, I was not afraid as I was in my childhood. Being tired and waiting long at the train stations, I often fell asleep. One night, I noticed the eyes of a vagabond staring at me. I was tired and rested my head on the bag in my arms while sitting on another bag and fell asleep. I trusted God that nothing bad would happen to me; I didn't even conjure up a frightful scene in my mind like I would have before.

I prayed to God asking Him to help me love my co-workers and especially my supervisor, whom I could not stand. I began to see the mistakes I had made before. I tried to understand my supervisor: what was it like to be in his shoes? He held a key position at our plant and held many responsibilities. He could not but notice the change in my attitude toward him.

The CEO eventually replaced my supervisor with another, younger person. Before he left, the supervisor treated us to a farewell lunch. Only a few hours had passed since we learned about the change in personnel, and yet my colleagues' attitude toward our former supervisor changed so quickly. I was shocked to see how disrespectful my colleagues suddenly became. They used to speak to him respectfully, even flattering him with near servility. For instance, they never dared to interrupt him. Now, they no longer waited for him to finish what he wanted to say. They talked to one another showing no sign of sympathy toward him, who was suffering due to the job change. Basically, they had taken off their masks. No doubt, he was well aware of this. In contrast, I did my best to make him feel respected. I spoke to him in a considerate manner. I asked him about the pride of his life—his grandson—and about his achievements. I think that was a revelatory moment for him. From then on, whenever we met in the lobby of the plant, our relationship resembled one of a daughter and her father.

God granted me favor with my new supervisor also. One of my tasks was to calculate bonuses for the workers. The proposals for the bonuses often came in at the last minute, and I had deadline to meet. I worked overtime, but on one occasion, I realized that I would have to work all night. I did not want anyone to learn about this.

Chapter 6   Back to the Village

I locked the door of the office thinking, *In the morning, I will be the first one who opens the door and no one will know*. I finished my work at dawn, and I was tired. I wanted to get some rest, so I joined two desks and I lay down on it. The "bed" was too stiff and hard for my back, but I had experience in that department! I woke up when someone tried to unlock the door. I went to the door; it was one of my co-workers.

"What were you doing? Did you sleep here?" she asked.

"Yes. I had to finish my work for the employees' bonus pay."

"I would have avoided doing such a thing at all costs. If I were you, I would have delayed the bonus payments."

Many others learned what I had done. One time my name was on the bonus list, too; the cashier made an error and brought less money than the total needed to distribute among the eligible employees. I told him, "I want to give up my bonus so that the next person on the list can have theirs." He did as I requested. However, this act did not go unnoticed by the payroll administrator, who then made a request for an additional bonus for me.

The last obstacle I remember experiencing in paying out the bonuses occurred with respect to the bank. One day my supervisor asked me to go with him and the cashier to the bank to withdraw the bonus money. Unfortunately, he had forgotten to make a withdrawal request the day before as was always required, and the payments were scheduled for the afternoon. The bank supervisor told us, "There is no way to get the money in such a short time."

My supervisor asked me, "What we going to do? Do we have to leave?" "No, we don't," I replied. "We will wait."

My confidence gave him courage as well. He and our cashier went to attend to other departments while I waited, praying. The bank supervisor moved on to work on something else that took precedence, but due to an unforeseen circumstance, he had to put the task on hold. He proceeded to work on our documents, and we returned to the plant with the money on time.

I wanted my fellow workers to view my faith in a more favorable light, not by persuasive words (anything that smacked of religious proselytizing was prohibited), but by deeds.

Alone for Christ

The fall came, and I wanted to bring my child home. I could not make those long travels in the winter. My baby already had an entire wardrobe, plus the crib. But how could I bring it all home? My parents did not allow any Adventists to come into the house. Therefore, the Samuels family arranged for a non-Adventist family to bring me my baby with everything he had.

Once my baby was home with me, I had no reason to leave. My mother had more opportunities to ridicule me. Her anger did not seem to have diminished at all. One day she hit me and pushed me. My head hit the glass door. The glass broke, but I had no cuts. My child became frightened, stood up in the crib, and started to cry. This compelled my mother to stop hitting me. She said, "Look at him! He wants to protect you."

The other day, my mother called a priest to convince me that I was wrong and to persuade me to return to the Orthodox Church.

The priest said, "The Orthodox Church has its origin in apostolic times. What about your church?"

"We are not saved by the church we belong to but by our personal relationship with God. Many of truths the first Christians believed have been lost and forgotten over the years. Some so-called Christian beliefs actually come from paganism, and most Christians don't know that. The Adventist Church came into existence out of the religious revival movements in the United States of America in 1844. The Adventist Church teaches strictly what the Bible says. God raised this church up with a special message to bring Christians back to the truths of the Bible, to prepare people for Jesus' second coming and the end of the world."

The priest looked mystified. He continued to cite tradition. When I quoted from the Bible, he quickly ended the discussion. He told my mother that I was irrecoverable, and left.

My mother refused to give up. She took my baby to an Orthodox church to ask another priest to baptize him into the Orthodox faith. The priest asked what the religion the baby's mother was. When he learned the mother was Adventist, he refused to baptize the child. I was grateful to that priest for his wisdom.

Mom, in a relentless effort to free me from this new religion, took some of my clothes to a witch who tried to "exorcise" the "demon" out of me.

I was scheduled for another trial of divorce, and I was not able to delay it anymore. It became clear to me there was no possibility for reconciliation. I learned that my husband was anxious to get a divorce because he wanted to remarry; his girlfriend was pregnant. To blame me he said was not able to conceive children. Well, God worked to bring the truth to the light.

Once I saw them together in his car while I was walking. I was hurt to see them happy. I felt betrayed, abandoned, forsaken, and rejected. But I did not hate him. After one year, the divorce ended with the following sentence: "the dissolution of marriage due to the exclusive fault of the wife." I would not have expected a different verdict during communism. I had to pay the court fees, which amounted to about two months' salary. I asked the court for permission to retain my husband's family name so that my son and I could share the same last name, but my husband refused it.

My only fear was losing my baby. I could finally breathe again when my child was entrusted to me by the court. But there was something else that most enraged my husband: "the apartment is awarded to the wife because she has to raise and educate the child and needs space."

I could not believe it; I got the apartment. I became free and could leave my parents' house! I lost my joy when I found out how much money I had to return to my husband in order to take sole possession of the apartment.

Alone for Christ

Emanuel at a year and a half.

I took out a loan from my work, but it was a small portion of the total funds needed. I borrowed money from several families from the church, but it was not enough. *Where am I going to get the balance?* From the people I least expected: Mom gave me her savings, and the highest amount I received came from my sister. I did not know when I could pay back all those who helped me.

I sent the money to my ex-husband. He did not bother to hand over the key, and I had to break the lock of the door. I went to court to ask the bailiff to come with me to get my share of common goods. He told me to come with a car. I went to a park near the courthouse and saw a man with a van; he was on his lunch break. I bargained with him for a ride, and, together we went to pick up the bailiff.

I arrived in front of the house that had been my home for four years. I learned that my sister-in-law's two-year-old daughter wept for a while and asked when I was coming back. My father-in-law confessed to an Adventist that he was sorry that I left, that it would have been better for them to have kept me even though I would not repent of my faith. We rarely appreciate something when we have it; we take it for granted.

My ex-husband led me to a warehouse where he kept my things. I did not expect my clothes to be in a warehouse. In addition, some of the things from my share were missing. But I took what he gave me and left. The driver unloaded everything in front of the building and left in a hurry. The bailiff was kind enough to keep a close watch on my belongings while I carried it up in batches in the elevator. After more than a year, I had finally taken possession of my clothes.

One day I received an envelope from the court; it was for another summons. I was ready to faint. My ex-husband was calling me in for a third trial because he was not satisfied with how our assets were distributed. He was asking me for half of the amount borrowed from his uncle when we purchased the apartment. In fact, he was asking for it a second time. That amount had already been included in the grand total.

I went to the trial without a lawyer because I could not afford one. I stated my case, convinced that the truth was as obvious as black and white. He had a lawyer and won the case. I realized what it means to have a lawyer. Is so good knowing we have an advocate in heaven—Jesus, who stands for us before God.

The amount I had to give my ex-husband was approximately one year's salary. Otherwise, he would take possession of the apartment.

I was so despondent. My trials came one after another for one and a half years. How was I to get this money, anyway? Sister Olson went with me to see Brother Adams, who had his own business. He said he would lend me the money once I received the court order. I received it on Thursday, and it stated that if I didn't pay by Monday, my ex-husband would take possession of the apartment.

I went to Brother Adams' work office. When he saw me at the door, his countenance changed. I knew I would not receive any money. I left saying, "You did not help me, but God will."

Where should I go and on which door should I knock? I searched through my house—what could I sell? I found a Persian rug, a wedding gift from my mother, but its value was only a tenth of the total amount I needed to come up with. However, I took the rug and went to another town where one of the church members lived. I had learned that she might be interested in this kind of rug. I did not remember her address very well. I knocked on a door, and Sister Gibson, her daughter, opened it. She told me her mother lived on another street.

Alone for Christ

"What business do you have with my mother?" she asked.

"I have a rug for sale."

Sister Gibson invited me in. She told me to wait until her husband came home. She saw how depressed I was and asked me what happened. I told her my situation and asked to rest somewhere. She led me to a room, where I fell asleep. I was drained from all the anxiety. When I woke up, she and her husband invited me to have dinner with them.

They were people with a modest lifestyle, and there was no hope that I could receive any help there. But God had indeed led me to the right people. They had just borrowed money from work to build a garage. They decided to give me the money and postpone the construction of the garage. It was exactly the amount I needed. I could not even give them any prospects or guarantees about when I could return the money. I paid the amount to my ex-husband, hoping that he would not bother me again.

Shortly afterwards, Brother Adams had an audit. In communism, this was tough. The auditors had been checking his ledgers for weeks, and he feared he would be sent to jail. Finally, he was required to pay a fine, which turned out to be three times higher than the money I asked to borrow. He came to the conclusion that God allowed him to lose money because he refused to lend to me.

Brother Samuels later learned that I had paid money to my ex-husband, and he appealed to the Supreme Court in Bucharest, where he could represent me. We won the appeal, and my ex-husband had to return the money.

I put myself in his shoes: *perhaps he no longer has the money*, I considered. *Perhaps he already invested the money*. I learned that he purchased an apartment. Therefore, I went to his parents' home to talk to his mother. I found her standing at the gate. I missed her and had the same affinity for her.

"How are you, Mom?"

She appeared thrilled that I still called her "Mom."

"I won the appeal in Bucharest and I have to get a refund. Maybe your son does not have the money anymore; I am willing to settle for the bedroom furniture in exchange." The furniture was valued at less than the refund, but I wanted to apply the Golden Rule: "So in everything, do to others what you would have them do to you, for this sums up the Law and the Prophets" (Matt. 7:12).

"We sold the furniture long ago, and you will get a refund." Then she turned around. I received the money and returned it to the Gibson family.

I cleaned my apartment. Sister Olson sold my bathroom set and tiles and purchased a refrigerator for me. Brother Adams gave me a used stove. Ian installed my doors, and Brother Carlson re-installed the tiles on the bathroom floor. When I finished making payments on the financing of the bedroom furniture, I purchased more furniture. The time came to replace the door with a real bed.

I was busy with work and church attendance. God blessed me with an extremely quiet child; I put him in day care. When he was home, he would play with the toys in his crib until he fell asleep.

One afternoon the power went off because I used my mini-electrical stove from my parents. It had happened once before, but my father was there at the time and adjusted something on the electric meter. I tried to do the same, but I could not. It was time to go to church. I prayed and flicked the light switch on in faith and left. When I returned in the evening, there was light in my apartment.

I will relate briefly other experiences around that time.

One night my son had a fever of over 40 degrees Celsius (104 Fahrenheit). I made compresses with vinegar but they did not work. I had no telephone to call a taxi and did not want to go out looking for a taxi with my child. It was dangerous to walk at night. I prayed and the child soon fell asleep and the next morning had no fever.

One Saturday when I took the bus to the church, I felt as if someone was looking through my purse. I searched for my wallet and it was missing. I knew that it did not contain any money, but my ID and transit pass were gone.

I prayed that I would recover my wallet by Monday, when I had to go to work. On Sunday my father came to visit me, and shortly after he arrived, someone knocked at the door. I looked through the peephole and saw a man. Had I been alone I would not have opened the door to a stranger. The man handed me the wallet, saying he found it discarded in the basement of a building. Absolutely nothing was missing.

Alone for Christ

One morning I missed the bus and had to ask a car driver for a ride. The driver told me his work place was close to my plant. When I got out of the car, I slammed the door, but my purse got caught in the door and remained attached to the car. I shouted to the driver, but he did not hear me and speeded off. I did not even have time to at least take down his license plate number.

Everything was in my purse: my ID, transit pass, and keys. I prayed to God to get my purse back by the end of my work day; otherwise, I could not enter my apartment. I struggled to maintain my trust in God that day. At the last minute, I got a call from security; the driver had brought my purse back. Apparently, when he arrived at his work place, his colleagues started to make fun of him because of the hanging purse. He remembered where he had dropped me off and came to my plant. The security then looked inside my purse and saw my ID.

To many people these stories may seem like nothing more than trifles, but to me these experiences are not at all trivial. Our lives consist of a sum of events, more or less significant. Having Jesus on my side, I understand all of these events as evidence of His love.

I acquired more friends at work than I had before my conversion. One of them was divorced, so we had something in common. Her daughter got into a car accident along with four other people, and she was the only one alive. However, she sustained serious injuries and was in the hospital. Her mother was in shock. I went to visit her along with two other co-workers. After a while, my colleagues left, but I stayed with her all night.

Another friend of mine had a large family and was often short on money. She asked me to lend some to her, knowing I am a believer. Her debt increased to half of her monthly salary. I thought about how difficult would be for her to pay me back. I therefore applied the Golden Rule and erased her debt.

But goodness is not always appreciated. Another workmate was alone; her husband had died a year earlier due to a work accident. She had no children and seemed sad, so I wanted to make her feel better. I invited her to my home. I purchased pizza and juice, and we ate together. I offered her some clothes, a pair of boots, and a matching purse. She stayed overnight, and the next day we went to the plant. But she did not report to work at her department. She missed five days without even calling, to the dismay of her supervisor. When she returned to work, she told a strange story: I invited her over and got her to sit on walnuts shells; then I gave her something to drink, and since then she had amnesia and could not remember anything. She lied to justify her absences.

I noticed how strangely her supervisor was looking to me. However, her colleagues did not believe her story and were disgusted by her lies. I was glad to know that there were some people who had their heads on straight. I especially appreciated the fact that those who knew me no longer considered that my church was a strange cult.

Chapter 7

Marriage

I took my vacation in the winter so I could stay home and study Ellen G. White books. I came to a point where my greater hunger and thirst were to know God.

My mother visited me one day and stayed overnight. In the morning I got up slowly and went to the living room to pray and study. My mother sensed that I had woken up, came to see what I was doing, and saw me on my knees. She jumped to the conclusion that I was crazy.

Sister Melon visited me one day and said, "Did you ever think that Emanuel needs a father?"

Old wounds rose to the surface, and I did not want to hear anything about it. But she was right: my child needed a father. Whenever I picked him up from day care, he did not take his eyes off from a father who used to come pick up his daughter.

I did not want to remarry. I would rather prefer to remain alone because I believed the end of the world was near. However, if God's will for me was otherwise, I would not dare to disregard it. I knelt to pray for a divine revelation of His will in this matter. Then, while I was praying with my eyes closed, an image of a young man appeared in my mind, of Gabriel from church. I stood up and said, "no way."

I knew Gabriel had not completed high school. I was worried about what others would think. I had made efforts to make them see me in a better light. I did not want to give them reasons to judge me again.

Moreover, Gabriel was not my type: he was tall and robust; I was petite and thin.

During communism, only a small number of Adventists managed to complete their higher education because the exams were often scheduled on Sabbath. I thought—and hoped—that God would choose one of them for me. However, I had a sense that God wanted me to take one more step downward on the ladder of humility. "Only God is able to humble us without humiliating us and to exalt us without flattering us."[1]

I told myself: *maybe I don't understand God's message quite right.* I did not bring this topic up in my prayers for six months, but I did not have peace. During church office elections, Gabriel and I were elected to serve in the youth department. Our paths began to cross; however, we did not have any occasions to really talk to each other yet.

I decided to pray to uncover God's will in this matter and to accept it. I prayed like never before to find God's direction for my life.

Thomas Merton, renowned American Catholic writer of the twentieth century, defined prayer as "an expression of who we are.... We are a living incompleteness. We are a gap, an emptiness that calls for fulfilment."[2]

I prayed and asked God to make His will absolutely clear so that I would not take a wrong turn. I read about Gideon who prayed using specified signs in order to know God's will. I decided to pray using two signs. The first sign I prayed for was that when I went to church Sabbath afternoon I would find Gabriel alone in the churchyard. The second was that when I started the conversation, Gabriel was to answer me kindly. Why did I ask to be the one to initiate the conversation? I realized he would not approach me knowing I had a bachelor's degree.

I was so nervous that Saturday afternoon. I could not stay home any longer, and I went to church earlier than usual. Did I find Gabriel in the churchyard? Yes, Gabriel was there, alone. I asked him whether he could give me some material to prepare a youth program. He agreed very kindly and offered to help me prepare the program.

The next moment, a mentally disabled sister appeared out of nowhere.

She started to walk around us and asked me, "Is he your husband?"

1   Ravi Zacharias, *Recapture the Wonder: Experiencing God's Amazing Promise of Childlike Joy* (Nashville, TN: Integrity Publishers, 2003), p. 118.
2   Philip Yancey, *The Jesus I Never Knew* (Grand Rapids, MI: Zondervan, 1995), p. 294.

Alone for Christ

Both of us were embarrassed. I was overwhelmed by an additional sign from God, and from then on, I simply waited to see how God would work to make this possible. I did not want to approach Gabriel to tell him that I had a revelation from God. I did not know that some girls or boys commonly made such claims and that this sentence was not credible anymore.

I noticed Gabriel would come to church with his mother. It seemed to me that it would be more honest to talk to both. I waited to see how God would create the opportunity for me to get to know his mother.

About a week passed, and his mother made an appeal in church to help a widow and her children in her village. Some members offered money, and I was the only one who offered to visit the widow. I took some clothes and food and went along with Gabriel's mother to visit her.

The widow had just become an Adventist, and she was sad that her oldest son ridiculed her faith and that his siblings followed suit.

I told these children my conversion story. The oldest son listened to me very intently; his siblings looked at him more than they did at me. I visited them several times together with Gabriel's mother. The Holy Spirit touched the boy, and he started to attend church. He ended up getting baptized and later served as an elder.

These witnessing occasions created a bond between Gabriel's mother and me. One day she invited me to her house. Her husband was not at home because he worked the night shift. I came in with great emotion. Gabriel was there, and I realized the time had come for me to tell them my secret.

It was such a struggle: How could I tell them? What would they think of me? It would sound as if I personally had my eyes on Gabriel. I decided that whatever the outcome, even if the whole community were to make fun of me as a result, I had to let it out because I could no longer bear the beating of my heart.

I collected myself and told them about how God had revealed to me that He had chosen Gabriel to be my husband. They were shocked. It was obvious they had never thought of me as a prospective wife. I did not ask for an answer; I only invited them to fast and pray together for three months for God to reveal His will to all of us.

They walked me to the bus stop. I later found out what they talked about on the way back.

"Gabriel, when this woman came to church for first time, the thought that crossed my mind was, 'she came for Gabriel.' " Gabriel's mother said to him.

"Mom, I had the same thought, but I did not tell you."

They started to put things together. Gabriel's mother recalled a dream she had: "she came in a room that looks like a store and a woman brought three flowers; one of them has bud and she chose that one." Gabriel's mother interpreted that dream as she chose a woman with a child.

Gabriel and his mom prayed about his marriage since he was fifteen years old. He was a good-looking man, and many girls from the church courted him. It was a mystery to everybody why he had not gotten married yet.

Because Gabriel and his mother could not discern God's will, she prayed that Gabriel's marriage would be like Isaac's (Genesis 24). She prayed, "Lord, make the girl come to us and then I will know who it is."

What embarrassed me so much was in fact an answer to her prayer. They did not need three months for clarification; even during the first month, we felt like we had known each other for a long time.

I learned that after Gabriel completed the first two years of high school, he and his mother were baptized. His father got very upset; his attitude was bad, especially toward his wife. Sometimes when they came back from church, the door was locked by his father. Gabriel dropped out of school and started to work to be able to take care of his mother in case his father ever kicked them out of their home. He then began taking classes in the evening and had two more years until his high school graduation.

He was a serious, spiritually focused individual and often gave presentations from the pulpit. I asked God to give me love for the one He had chosen for me. And then one day, I saw him as I never had before; he looked like an angel to me. I felt my heart getting warmer, and I knew God had poured into me a heavenly love for Gabriel.

It seemed like my vision was blurred. I hadn't noticed at first how handsome he was—that's why so many girls courted him. I began to see his kindness, sincerity, and transparency.

Alone for Christ

He reminded me of an incident that took place at church. My father came in during the sermon and began to shout: "Folks, get this woman out of here because she abandoned her husband."

Gabriel confessed to me that he felt a deep desire to take me home with him so that I would not be persecuted anymore. We began to enjoy a wonderful friendship. I thought it would stay that way for a while. I figured he was busy with work and school and so we were going to marry after his graduation. His mother thought the same. But surprise! He announced to us the wedding date. I loved that he had taken the initiative. I realized God wanted us to get married sooner than I thought. At that point, only three months had passed since our first discussion.

His mother opened her wardrobe and showed me all the many beautiful clothes she had kept for her future daughter-in-law. She had a cousin in Germany from whom she received clothes. Surprisingly, the clothes were my size. I always liked good-quality clothes, but I had never been better dressed than I was now.

All of us realized our wedding would have some obstacles. We had to notify the pastor and board; they could think we were rushing the wedding. If they were to ask me how I knew this was God's will, what would I tell them? My experience with signs from God could be considered subjective, irrelevant or contrived.

I searched the Bible for any passages I could rely on for support. I read Genesis chapter 24 about the marriage between Isaac and Rebekah. At the time I did not know Gabriel's mother had prayed for things to flow according to the story in that passage. Here is what I found:

Verses 13 and 14: "See, I am standing beside this spring, and the daughters of the townspeople are coming out to draw water. May it be that when I say to a girl, 'Please let down your jar that I may have a drink' and she says 'drink, and I'll water your camels too'—let her be the one you have chosen for your servant Isaac. By this I will know that you have shown kindness to my master." Abraham's servant, Eliezer, left to find a young lady for Isaac and asked for a sign: if she speaks kindly, she is the one. Rebekah spoke kindly to Eliezer and offered more than he asked. And so in verse 19, "After she had given him a drink, she said, 'I'll draw water for your camels too.' " It was the same with Gabriel: he offered me not only the material for the youth program but his help, too.

Verse 21: "Without saying a word, the man watched her closely to learn whether or not the Lord had made his journey successful." Similar to Eliezer, I did not reveal anything to Gabriel until after the fulfillment of my requested signs. I waited to see how God would work.

Verse 33: "Then food was set before him but he said, 'I will not eat until I have told you what I have to say.'" I confided my secret only once I had the opportunity to be at Gabriel's house in his mother's presence.

Verse 50: "Laban and Bethuel answered, 'This is from the Lord, we can say nothing to you one way or the other.'" In my story also, both Gabriel and his mother later confirmed that my proposal was from God.

Verse 58: "So they called Rebekah and asked her, 'Will you go with this man?'" When Gabriel became certain that God had chosen me to be his wife, he gladly accepted the divine plan.

Verse 53: "Then the servant brought out gold and silver jewelers and articles of clothing and gave them to Rebekah." In addition to clothing, Gabriel's mother also gave me household items from Germany.

Verses 55 and 56: "But her brother and her mother replied, 'Let the girl remain with us ten days or so; then you may go.' But he said to them, 'Do not detain me, now that the Lord has granted success to my journey. Send me on my way so I may go to my master.'" Gabriel's mother and I could wait another "ten days" after the graduation, but not Gabriel. He did not want to wait any longer and booked the wedding date.

I was amazed to discover the many similarities between this biblical marriage and ours. We invited Pastor Michael to officiate at our wedding, and he was convinced by those seven similarities.

What about Gabriel's father? I was nervous to meet him. What was he going to say when he found that his son wanted to marry a woman who already had a child? Wouldn't he blame the "strange faith" of his son? And yet, on the contrary, Gabriel's father liked me from the very first moment and especially my child.

What would my parents' reaction be? When my mother saw Gabriel, she exclaimed, "You are the man who guarded the door to keep me away at Marinela's baptism."

Alone for Christ

I did not know this until then, and this helped me see God's providence even more. I finally came to the understanding as to why God had brought me back to my hometown: to meet Gabriel.

My mother continued, "Hey, Gabriel, couldn't you find another girl? You have never been married, but she has, and she has a child…"

God often does things contrary to human reason. "The man without the Spirit does not accept the things that come from the Spirit of God, for they are foolishness to him, and he cannot understand them, because they are spiritually discerned" (1 Cor. 2:14).

However, the opposition came from elsewhere. When we announced the date of our engagement, one of the girls who liked Gabriel became very angry. She got his phone number from work and called him a few times. She was determined to change his mind. She told him she would make fun of him whenever he was seen with a baby and a short wife. Gabriel resisted her harassment.

One of the men from church who had a degree approached me. He got my phone number from work and called me. He did not clearly tell me what he wanted; what I understood was that he visited my parents. I wondered why. I agreed to meet with him after work.

He brought me a small bunch of flowers, so it was not difficult to guess his intentions. He started to talk about himself: he was divorced (although he did not have biblical grounds for divorce), had a child who remained with his ex-wife, graduated from college, had such a position at work, etc. Then he started to denigrate Gabriel: he did not have a degree, etc. I stopped him: "You have a child who needs his father. I know how hard it is to be a single mom. And you dare to come to me and denigrate Gabriel, who is a noble man? Moreover, you visited my parents to influence them against my marriage? This is the end of our discussion."

I threw his flowers away and left. I had learned a lesson: a Christian must be not only gentle but firm as well.

Gabriel's mother had her trial, too. She was scorned several times by the women in her village. "You have only one son and you are marrying him to a divorced woman with a child instead of a virgin!"

Gabriel's mother answered them: "Don't you worry. A virgin is a woman the day after."

Finally, our wedding day came. I had planned to go to the hairdresser that morning. The Adventist women styled their hair. I had long hair but no skill to style it. When I was ready to leave my apartment, my sister came. I planned to spend some time with her and put a Christian music cassette to play. Her reaction was not what I expected; she hurled insults and demeaning remarks and left angry. I was so sad because she missed the wedding. I wanted my wedding to be an opportunity for her to hear a sermon and to change her prejudice against Adventists.

I visited a couple of hair salons, and it was clear that if I waited in line, that wedding day would be one without a bride. I came back home thinking I would ask a sister from church to arrange my hair somehow. Soon there was a knock at the door from three families—they were Gabriel's relatives. It was the first time we met, and I was embarrassed they did not find me styling my own hair. How did they find me? They wanted to go to church but did not know where the church was and took a taxi to the bride's address.

To my surprise, one of Gabriel's cousins worked as a hairdresser. God sent a hairdresser home to me! What a wonderful God we have! How He attends to even the insignificant details of our lives.

The time came for Gabriel and I to stand before the altar in the church sanctuary. Pastor Michael started to preach: "And because the midwives feared God, he gave them families of their own" (Exod. 1:21). At that time, the chances to marry someone within the church were slimmer; there were fewer boys than girls. But God provided me a family. The pastor ended his sermon: "The glory of this present house will be greater than the glory of the former house,' says the Lord Almighty. 'And in this place I will grant peace,' declares the Lord Almighty" (Hag. 2:9).

Gabriel and Marinela at their wedding

It was a beautiful wedding. With my hand in Gabriel's hand, I felt like my steps were landing in the clouds.

Elder Parker told Gabriel, "You waited, but you got it." "As for me, the kingdom of heaven began," I said.

Elder Parker tried to temper me, saying that this did not mean there would be no problems. But by now I could say the same thing. After three years of trials that exhausted me, God provided a husband and protector for me. My marriage gave me the comfort and peace that I had longed for such a long time. In addition, I gained two wonderful parents. My relationship with my mother-in-law resembled the relationship between Naomi and Ruth.

I was curious to see my son's reaction. I cannot describe it in words— he was so happy. At two years and two days old, God gave him a father.

Oh, how they played together.

One night, while we were sleeping, I felt a weight. I opened my eyes and saw my son peacefully sleeping above us. I woke Gabriel and asked him, "Did you take him out of the crib?"

"No."

Emanuel had not climbed out of his crib before. We pulled him out in front of us. He moved his head back and forth, looking at me and at Gabriel. From then on, it was always a challenge to get him to sleep in his crib. Everywhere we went, he was in Gabriel's arms. At church he hardly moved, perfectly happy and content to be in his dad's arms.

Gabriel wanted to adopt my son. My ex-husband was never interested in seeing the child. One day my ex-husband had this opportunity. I was walking with Emanuel, and he was coming from the opposite direction. When he was close enough to recognize me, he abruptly changed his direction and entered into a restaurant lot.

I called my ex to tell him about the adoption. He felt relieved, as his obligation to pay child support would come to an end. During the adoption process, the clerk warned me that it was not wise to have my child adopted by a man without a degree. She told me I did not realize what this would entail. She was reasoning as most people would have. In communism, vanity was prevalent. For the most part, character, moral integrity, and loyalty did not matter to people.

When the adoption process was complete, we were all so happy to be sharing the same family name. My son's past was replaced by a new, more promising identity. When we ask God to lead our lives, we will find immeasurable joy.

Another gift from Gabriel was that I could stay home and take care of our child. I had reached a point where I was no longer able to replace working on Saturdays with guard nights. My supervisor tried his best to cover me, but the CEO learned about this situation and was unwilling to tolerate a person in his company who did not work on Saturday.

When I returned from our honeymoon, I told my supervisor that I was resigning. He urged me to stay.

"I cannot get Saturdays off in exchange for guard nights anymore."

"Don't worry; I'll cover you."

"I do not want the CEO to find out and create problems for you."

"Let me deal with the CEO."

Alone for Christ

My supervisor was new and inexperienced with respect to the CEO; the former supervisor was replaced by the CEO even though he had a lot of experience and good working relationships with people in high positions.

I asked my supervisor to accept my resignation. At that time the law had an article that was favorable to terminating work in order to take care of children under seven years old. This article did not prevent subsequent employment elsewhere. Three years since my conversion had passed, and I terminated my work in the most honorable way.

I had more to discover about Gabriel's generosity. While he was working, he saved some money to buy a car, but he used his money to pay all my loans instead.

We enjoyed living together and visited his parents very often. They lived in the country in a house with three rooms and a bathroom. Emanuel enjoyed playing outside. Gabriel's father was a surly man, but he changed for the sake of his grandson. Emanuel would sleep in his arms or next to him and used to cup his cheeks in his palms until he fell asleep.

For the first time in my life, I felt at home in their home. Gabriel used to go there for his lunch break and would go to school after work. Actually, we saw each other only in the morning and at night. To keep the apartment for much longer did not make any sense. We concluded that it would be better to sell our apartment and move in with Gabriel's parents.

However, moving from the city to the country was considered a crazy, nonsensical move at the time. My parents now had new reasons to criticize me. We prayed and waited on God's will. Interestingly enough, sales of apartments had been stopped by communism; and then, more recently, the purchases were. Overriding the system was impossible for us.

One of my neighbors wanted to buy my apartment for his parents to move into. They happened to have favorable connections with people in high positions, and three months later succeeded to get their purchase approved.

I applied the Golden Rule in dealing with them as well. I offered to sell at the price that I had originally paid for the apartment even though its market value had doubled. Any other person could have taken advantage of this, but not God's child. I knew they had the money and wanted my apartment and no other. But I wanted to testify of how God wants to do business. I considered that maybe this might be their only opportunity to meet an Adventist, and I wanted to leave a good impression.

We purchased a one-year-old car of the Romanian make Dacia. Thanks to vendor relationships, we got a license plate bearing three digits. During communism, regular plate numbers had four digits; the three-digit plate numbers were assigned only to people with a recognized communist status or well paid jobs. Having this type of plate meant you would rarely be stopped by a police officer.

Driving one day, we happened to pass my ex-husband's car. I imagined how amazed he must have been to see we had a three-digit license plate as he did. My ex-mother-in-law had said about me, "she will never have a car." Poor humans. How falsely bold they are to make predictions for the future.

A week after we sold our apartment, the revolution began and communism fell. A new era of democracy was established, which changed many things. Some institutions were abolished. One of them was the Economic Militia, where my ex-husband had aspired to get in. Also, the value of the currency dropped drastically. Thank God we had sold the apartment prior to this. Religious freedom and a work week of five days were some of the good changes that came out of democracy.

Then one of my former coworkers contacted me. Gabriel and I visited her. She became interested in religion, and we began studying the Bible together. After some time, she and her daughter were baptized. Her daughter had just been nominated as the most beautiful girl at the high school banquet. Had they not met Jesus at that time, perhaps the daughter's future would now be different. Her encounter with Christ put her feet on the path of seriousness and responsibility. They moved to another European country, where her husband was baptized, too. The daughter graduated with two college degrees and married a pastor, with whom she entered into a happy marriage. God honors those who honor Him.

Two years passed since my wedding. During this time, I was resting from all my trials. "Praise be to the Lord, who has given rest to his people Israel just as he promised." (1 Kings 8:56). But now it was time to get off the emotional highs and lows and discover what God had for me to do. I did have a desire to serve God and submitted my résumé to the Seventhday Adventist Union. One year later, my husband and I attended the first evangelistic conference organized after the fall of communism. The speakers were from the Euro-Africa Division. We drove our car together with Pastor Maier and his wife. We basked in a week filled with spirituality.

Alone for Christ

It was a rainy day and the road was slippery on our way back when Pastor Maier drove the car. Suddenly he stepped on the brake to avoid a collision, and our car began to slide and careened off the road, crashing into a tree. We escaped with minor scratches, but our car was seriously damaged and had to be towed.

When we arrived home without the car, my in-laws were pretty scared, and my mother-in-law hesitated to tell us about a telegram. It was from the union asking me to come for an interview the next day.

I felt that this was God's call, and I immediately took the train to Bucharest. "The opportunity to use whatever gifts you have in the service of the Lord of the Gift is the chance of a lifetime. But it will slip away from you unless you are very intentional. The time to respond is *at once*."[3]

The Adventist union had purchased their first personal computer (PC) and was going to hire someone. They saw in my résumé that I had graduated from the Faculty of Cybernetics. Now I knew why I had decided years earlier to attend none other than this faculty.

I used to work on Romanian computers, a brand called Felix, where data was entered using punched cards. I had never seen a PC, and after communism fell, PCs where imported from abroad. I prayed for God to give me the skills required to work a PC. After a few weeks' training, I started to work on typing, editing and typesetting biblical studies, the quarterly Adventist magazine *Signs of the Times*, and other ongoing programs.

I really loved what I was doing. However, it was a lot of work, and I worked overtime on a daily basis. The computer monitor was of a poor quality, and my eyes would burn due to the radiation, but I was happy to work for God.

Even though I worked hard, I did not received any money. I didn't bring it up because I did not know whether they had hired me. One month passed, then two and three. I travelled to see my family every weekend, and I would go back to work with money and some food. One of my aunts hosted me for free. She had been observing my life since my conversion, and her prejudices against Adventists went away.

---

3   John Ortberg, *If You Want to Walk on Water, You've Got to Get Out of the Boat* (Grand Rapids, MI: Zondervan, 2001), p. 40.

Our car was still being serviced; Pastor Maier paid his part, but our car needed additional expensive repairs. At the end of the third month, the treasurer asked me, "How much have you received on your paycheck?"

"Nothing."

He called the accountant and told him to pay me retroactively. I realized this situation happened due to someone's negligence. But God had allowed it for a purpose: I received a lump sum for the three unpaid months, which covered the entire car repair.

In His wisdom, God knows better as to what we need and when we need it. An old Hasidic story says that everyone must wear a coat with two pockets for receiving messages from God. In one pocket God's note read, "You are just one of the millions of grains of sand in the universe." In the note in the other pocket, He wrote, "I made the entire universe just for you."

The union purchased several other PCs, and I offered to train all who wanted to learn to work on a PC. For this purpose, an improvisational classroom was conducted in the hallway. When the students went home, I continued to work overtime.

After three more months, my husband joined me in God's work at the Seventh-day Adventist Union. We moved in with another aunt, who gave us our own room. It was unbelievable how two of my relatives welcomed me, "the black sheep" of my family. The aunt lived on the outskirts of Bucharest. She had a well in the yard and no bathroom or heat. That's why we left Emanuel in the care of my in-laws.

A few months later, I had a challenge before me. God uses challenges to develop our ability to trust Him. The division's auditors came to introduce the bookkeeping software. The union had three bookkeepers who worked manually. Having accounting and computer knowledge, I was appointed to operate the computerized bookkeeping.

God led me to this position. I found my vocation and calling. Speaking about the meaning of a calling, Frederick Buechner wrote, "This is the place where your deep joy meets the world's deep need."[4] It does not mean that you will have only joy when you follow your calling. Many times you have to prove your determination when it would be easier to quit. When you are chosen for a job and gifted by God Himself to perform it, this divine encounter gives you strength to go forward.

---

4   Frederick Buechner, *Wishful Thinking: A Seeker's ABC* (San Francisco, CA: Harper-One, 1993), p. 119.

Alone for Christ

I figured out why our car accident occurred the day before my interview. The devil wanted to prevent me from joining God's work. During troublesome times we should be able to discern a message directed to us. Hellen Keller (June 27, 1880–June 1, 1968), the first deaf and blind person who got a degree in arts said, "Character cannot be developed in ease and quiet. Only through experience of trial and suffering can the soul be strengthened, ambition inspired, and success achieved."

The accounting software was in French, and I had to overcome the language barrier. Another challenge was waiting for me right around the corner: one of the accountants retired, the second one got married in another town, and the third one moved to the Adventist publishing house. I did not have enough time to learn from their experience.

I had to do the work of all three of them: the bookkeeping of the union, the pension fund, and the theological institute. I worked overtime to cover everything. During my work, I felt the Holy Spirit speaking to me and teaching me what to do.

It was late fall when our room gradually got colder. Right then, one of the union directors moved from a one-bedroom apartment into a house. The housing for the union staff was provided by the union. The free apartment was then given to us and we could bring Emanuel home to live with us.

I kept on working overtime, and my husband would bring Emanuel to work after kindergarten. He used to play until he fell asleep on a chair but was happy to be with us.

The division auditors were satisfied with the work I was doing and offered me to go to France to work as bookkeeper for an Adventist nonprofit organization. I could bring my family, but the offer for work was only for me. I felt that I could not leave behind my work in Romania and did not take time to ask God about it. I declined the offer.

The union purchased PCs for its six conferences, and I trained their accountants for the same accounting software. My work load increased even more when the union commenced the construction of the theological institute campus.

Although I worked very much, I did it with all my heart, knowing that I worked for God. Ellen G. White had much to say about the satisfaction that one always gets in God's work; I confess that I always got this satisfaction.

We were given the opportunity to build a house on some land inherited by my father-in-law. It was a parcel located on the outskirts of his native village near the forest. The village was small, with old houses and no sewage.

First, we wanted to plant corn on the land. It was a long drive, and we needed a place to rest. This is how the house project was born.

Gabriel's mother was half-German and had many capabilities necessary for the project and started building the house. The village people had never seen a woman working at construction. We helped her when on vacation, and it took a few years, but we did finish the house and fence in the land. It was the most beautiful house in the village and was known as the house built by a woman. Maybe that's why people accepted the religious literature that my mother-in-law offered them.

Gabriel's dream was to study theology. The opportunity came in the way of part-time courses. While I inquired about enrollment, the Adventist Theological Institute's director asked me, "Why don't you register along with him?"

"Can women enroll, too?"

"Yes, it is the first time we are admitting women into theology."

We enrolled together and passed the admission exam. We had to study theology for five years. I wondered how and when I would manage to learn with my overloaded schedule.

God was in charge of that. The construction of the institute was completed, and this created new job opportunities. I trained an accountant for the institute; a few months later, I trained another one for the pension fund. As a result, I did not have to work overtime and had time to study. We really liked what we studied. When we were in the middle of studying for exams, we needed two separate rooms because each of us needed space to learn out loud. During that time our son would do his homework in the bathroom.

Studying at the seminary helped us develop a balanced understanding of theological subjects and avoid the extremes in religion. The day of our graduation marked a fall of another wall of opposition my family had against my faith. I had not become an idiot as they assumed, but succeeded in graduating from yet another faculty. In addition, nobody could say anymore that I married a man without a bachelor's degree.

Alone for Christ

In the meantime, the union started constructing its new buildings. I had the financial audits from the government on a quarterly basis. This caused me much stress. However, I felt rewarded by the very work that I was doing. God had an even better reward in store for me. I was offered the position of assistant treasurer, and we moved into a bigger house. It was two-bedroom semi-detached house. The only inconvenience was having to access the bathroom through our child's bedroom. But more importantly, we had a small yard where our son could play.

One day he was in a bad mood and told me, "Mommy, I do not have enough space to play in the yard because the car is there."

How was I to answer him? Had I said, "Play along with it," he wouldn't have been satisfied and would have continued to bug me about it all day long. If I were to have asked my husband to pull the car out into the street, we would have created a precedent. Children often puzzle you with their questions.

I replied, "We are going to sell it some day."

He did not like my answer because he was looking forward to growing up and getting his driver's license. Therefore, he left quickly without a complaint and had "enough" space to play. I found that humor was an effective technique in my child's education.

Speaking of cars, I would like to share some more experiences. Seven years passed since we bought our first car. We spent a lot of money on repairs. We wanted to sell it and buy another one but did not have enough money.

My mother-in-law's cousin from Germany invited us to visit them. It was the first time I had the opportunity to visit another country and saw the difference between our ex-communist country and others.

Our relatives paid our bus fare and offered us some Deutsche Marks (German currency). Our boy received one Mark each time he led the buggy through the store.

We returned to work on a Monday, when I found out that the car loan had been increased. On that day Gabriel went to the workshop to have our car repaired and found that the mechanic urgently needed money and wanted to sell his car that week. Sunday was the only day to go to a used car fair. But we prayed and found a customer for our car on Thursday.

On Friday we bought the car from the mechanic and joyfully drove to Gabriel's village. As we approached his parents' house, our child and his grandma were sitting outside the gate. Gabriel slowed down. They did not recognize the car and probably wondered, *What is going on with that driver?*

To their surprise, it was we who got out of the car. Our son was especially surprised and happy. We told them how wonderfully God had worked things out. None of details were overlooked so that the achievements can all be attributed to a praise-worthy God. I felt as if I was always in God's hands, defended from all of the evils outside.

Dacia cars—the Romanian make—would wear quickly and swallow money on repairs. There is a Romanian saying: "With a Dacia you will know only two joys—when you buy it and when you sell it. In between, you have only trouble!"

In any case, Gabriel concluded it would be better to buy a new Dacia. We hoped to cover the cost of the new one from the sale of our old car and the car loan from work. We planned to do that upon returning from the holiday.

First, Gabriel went to an automotive service shop for an inspection and tune-up and had new brakes put in. Then we left for vacation to the union's resort. To our dismay, during our drive back home, a car in front of us braked suddenly. My husband slammed on the brakes, but the car did not slow down. Gabriel swerved to the left. An oncoming truck that had just gotten moving on the road struck my door and propelled our car into a rock. Luckily, none of us sustained any injuries. The road workers pulled our car back on the road. The car was damaged but was still running. We went to the police station to report the accident. A police officer then accompanied us to an automotive shop to confirm that the brakes did not in fact work. We were very puzzled to discover that one of the pads did not even exist. Had Gabriel not been present at our car inspection and witnessed the brake installation, he would have agreed with the police officer that the mechanic had forgotten to put one in! It was inexplicable.

We were running out of time. Our relatives from Germany had just come to the Black Sea, and we wanted to reward their hospitality by offering ours. We needed a car to go with them to the seaside resorts, but now our car was broken. Fixing it could take many days; that meant not having a car during our relatives' holiday.

Alone for Christ

We prayed for a miracle, namely for the car dealer to buy our damaged car and sell us a new one. I called the work place and learned that the car loan had just been increased. We changed our route and drove to the dealer at a snail's pace. Things went just the way we prayed, and the following day we drove to Gabriel's parents in a new Dacia. Once again we surprised them, and this time our child was our acolyte.

Time passed with typical joys and sorrows of daily life. But we felt that with our God we could overcome any mountain. "With your help I can advance against a troop; with my God I can scale a wall" (2 Sam. 22:30).

Chapter 8

Disappointment

I experienced the euphoria that new converts feel in their fresh walk with God when He answers their prayers almost immediately. Problems are easily overcome. You are on top! However, the time eventually came for me, as it does to all converts, to come back down to a station called "reality." You come to discover some inner things that you cannot beat as easily. Also, you discover that some of the things that you thought were behind you can resurface. It is God's way of telling you can never be selfsufficient and that you have to grow up.

Charlotte Ishkanian, editor of the *Adventist Mission* magazine, published my conversion story. The magazine was translated into the Romanian language, and the missionary news were being read in church. My story had to be read over two Sabbaths.

One Sabbath I visited the church where I was baptized. I expected that they would give me an opportunity to share my experience with the congregation. Not only did this not happen, but the Sabbath School superintendent did not want the missionary news to be read at all. He knew that my story happened to be up next in the readings and I was present. I later learned about the discussions that took place.

"What do you mean you don't want the missionary news to be read up front?" someone objected.

It was time for the Sabbath School team to go to the pulpit, and they delayed. I prayed, sensing that something was going on. Finally, a girl who received the booklet at the last minute read my experience in an awkward fashion. This grieved me.

Alone for Christ

We came back to the same church the next Sabbath. The second part of the article telling my story, which was scheduled to be read that day, was once again overlooked. I sat on a chair listening to someone who read my experience in a boring monotonous way. I felt like a composer who had to sit on a chair and listen to his song being played by a beginner. However, I received some consolation. Charlie Chaplin had a worse experience. He went to a competition that awarded contestants who could best imitate Charlie Chaplin. All the contestants were dressed and made to resemble him, but Charlie himself, of course, did not need to disguise anything or do anything to look the part! He entered the competition and placed third.

Well, the years went by, and our son reached high school age. We prayed and fasted with him to find out God's will for him. One of my coworkers told me about an international high school of computer science that taught in English. I said, "No way. We cannot afford to send him to a private high school due to the fees."

"You should think more about it," my colleague insisted.

Her words stirred me. *Does God want to tell me something?* I talked to Gabriel, and he seemed ready for any sacrifice. I asked Emanuel, "Would you like to learn computer science in a private high school?"

"Oh, yes! But we don't have money."

"If this is God's will, He will provide."

I called to ask about the fees; they were less than I had expected. We visited the school and were pleased with its equipment. However, the following was going to be a challenge: the admission exams in mathematics and English, plus a psychological test.

That year Emanuel focused on the subjects he would be tested on in the mandatory graduation exam, which was used to rank the students for public high school admission. Based on the marks on the graduation exam, a student could be accepted by one of the high schools.

However, we thought that taking the private high school's admission exams was worth a try. I accompanied Emanuel to the exam. All three tests were on the same day. I was waiting with other parents; they were wealthy, full of themselves, and spoke English fluently. What chance did we have to compete with upper-class people?

104

Chapter 8   Disappointment

At the end of the exams, my boy came out looking discouraged. I went to see the results: aside from the students who were admitted and those who were rejected, two were classified as "reserves": another student and Emanuel. I asked the secretary what this meant, and she explained to me that if one of the admitted students withdrew, then one of the reserves take that student's place.

I could not imagine why someone who passed the exam would want to withdraw afterward. In addition, even if this were to happen, the first reserve on the list would be contacted, not Emanuel. However, I thought, *God has not yet given His last word on the matter*.

The days passed, and I was expecting a phone call from any high school to find about my son's admission. To my surprise, however, I received a call from the private high school secretary, who asked me to come with one hundred dollars to enroll Emanuel because someone had withdrawn. Why the other reserve was not called instead, I did not know. All I knew was that God had a plan for Emanuel to better learn English. And so, Emanuel attended the private computer science high school even though the chances of that happening had been slim in our perception.

During his high school years, we became friends with two of his Muslim teachers. They were very open in their approach to the subject of religion. In fact, in my experience, Muslims tend to speak more easily about their religion than do Christians about theirs; sometimes Christians can be rather reluctant to confess their beliefs. To learn how to approach the Muslim teachers, I studied a booklet entitled *How to approach Muslims*. I read something about their teachings from the Koran. Whenever we met, we were careful to emphasize points that our religions held in common. At their request, we offered them some study materials. They were sincere seekers of truth, and we believed that God's Spirit would guide them. We were thankful for the opportunity to build bridges and leave things in God's hands.

As for us, God kept blessing us and carrying us through various difficulties. We had expected that after the fall of communism, life would significantly improve, but this was not so. Inflation raised the cost of living continually. Our wages did not keep up with inflation, and we lived from a paycheck to a paycheck.

Alone for Christ

Eventually, Gabriel's parents retired, but the pensions were small. My mother-in-law got ill, and so we brought her home with us. She had to have treatment for two years, which was costing us more than we could afford. We started to sell items such as the piano, furniture, and books to pay for her treatment. Then my father-in-law got sick, and we paid for his surgery.

As for my parents, they still had not changed their attitude toward me after all these years. Despite seeing our good marriage and God's evident hand in our lives, my parents did not stop criticizing me about my religion. When a person holds on to certain prejudices, he or she literally refuses to see the evidence.

For instance, my mother objected to the fact that Seventh-day Adventists did not practice offering feasts for the dead as was commonly practiced in the Orthodox religion. My mother complained that my religion would one day inevitably prevent me from offering food as charity at her gravesite. My mother was very conscientious about offering food for the dead according to Orthodox tradition. They did not see that the notion of human consciousness after death could not be justified in the Bible; it had pagan origins. "For the living know that they will die, but the dead know nothing; they have no further reward, and even the memory of them is forgotten" (Eccl. 9:5).

Furthermore, nothing I accomplished was enough to satisfy my parents. They kept on reproaching me and calling me a loser. In their minds, I could not possibly gain any possessions in life due to my religion. They saw my faith as a barrier to all the superficial things they valued.

People are fascinated and mesmerized by the outward, material, superficial things and overlook the spiritual dimension of life. I did not focus on material things. All I wanted was a decent living, but my parents' long-held disdain plagued me. I wished I could have enough money to give to my parents. I began to think that perhaps God could use this to wipe out their last argument against my faith.

When my father reached the age of seventy, I wept because my childhood dream to delight my father with fried chicken had not yet been fulfilled. I had bought him only the wristwatch. Someone once said, "the death of our dreams does not mean the death of God's promises." I tried to find comfort in that.

106

Sadly, however, the outbursts of anger, resentment, and reproach from my parents continually exasperated me. In the meantime, my husband and I were experiencing financial constraints. These were very trying times.

Almost simultaneously with these trials came another one: spiritual crisis. I took my eyes off Jesus. We, as human beings, cannot look in two places at the same time. If we look at people, it means we have directed our vision away from God. But if you must look at God through a man, then look at Him through the man Jesus Christ. He is the only one who represented God as He is.

I began to doubt God's love for me. Doubts have more to do with feelings than with the intellect. In his book *In Step With God*, Charles Stanley writes:

> Feelings have nothing to do with the Christian life. They change. One moment you may "feel" close to God, and the next hour or so you don't. You think, "What has happened? Has He left me?" No. He never changes, He never leaves and He never abandons you. One of the enemy's favorite methods of operation is to tempt us into feeling a certain way that is nowhere near reality. What is true? The unconditional love of God. What is unshakeable? The love of God. What is the one thing that will never change? His love for you and me.[1]

One night as my middle brother was coming out of a club, he was followed by two men who assumed he was someone else and stabbed him to death. A few years later my father died at the age of seventy-three, and that's when my anger toward God began. I thought my father and middle brother died without being reconciled to God and were lost forever. In contrast, I had read accounts of other persons who came to God and faced opposition in their families but whose family members eventually joined the faith. The fact that no one from my family came to God was proof of my failure as a Christian, I thought. It meant that I did not pray enough or that my life did not speak convincingly enough about my faith.

My mother told me one day, "Marinela, you are so stupid. I read in the Bible, too, that 'a man can do nothing better that to eat and drink and find satisfaction in his work' (Eccl 2:24). So, go eat and drink and do not

---

1   Charles F. Stanley, *In Step With God: Understanding* (Nashville, TN: Thomas Nelson, 2008), p. 220.

pursue 'green horses on the walls' anymore. I agree with Ecclesiastes: 'I have seen all the things that are done under the sun; all of them are meaningless, a chasing after the wind' " (Eccl. 1:14).

I marveled at my mother's out-of-context conclusion after reading the book Ecclesiastes instead of taking heed to the conclusion of the book itself: "Here is the conclusion of the matter: fear God and keep his commandments, for this is the whole duty of man. For God will bring every deed into judgment, including every hidden thing, whether it is good or evil" (Eccl. 12:13, 14).

I knew that actions spoke louder than words, and so I thought I could give the best testimony by providing for them financially. I was angry that God did not bless me financially. I knelt and said in prayer as the apostle Peter once did: "We have left everything to follow! What then will there be for us?" (Matt. 19:27). Pastor Nick Butoi once said in a sermon: "One of the temptations of those who suffer persecution for their faith is that they think they are entitled to special privileges as a kind of compensation. When these things do not occur as they think it should be, then the disappointment comes."

I felt an abyss under my feet, and I was ready to tumble in. When I was under attack from my ex-husband, my family, and my work, I knew where to run: to God. But now, when it seemed as if God was letting me down, where could I go? New trials came, and I cried out wondering whether God even cared about me anymore. Things did not turn out as I had hoped and dreamt. What the psychologist Carl Jung once said resonated with me: "I know that I am never more tempted than when my life does not go as I planned."[2]

I started to lose my joy on the path of faith. I was so desperate. I continued to pray and study but felt that nothing was helping me. This was the devil's way to target and attack my faith. *Should I continue to trust in God or not? Does God still care of me, or not? What am I in His eyes?* Waves of doubts flooded my mind. I could see nothing else on the horizon other than my aging and failure to financially help my loved ones.

I did not entrust these fears to God's care, and, as a result, I lost His peace. Dallas Willard wrote: "I meet many Christians who, despite their belief, are deeply disappointed by the evolution of their lives. Often, due

---

2   Carl Jung, *Collected Works of C. G. Jung* (Princeton, NJ: Princeton University Press, 1973), Vol. 2, p. 75

to the circumstances or bad decisions and actions of others, they failed to achieve in life what they had hoped. This makes them struggle, thinking they have done something wrong or doubt that God was really with them."[3]

But praise be to God; He helped me come to my senses. I could not at once throw overboard all that I believed or my experiences with God. From that moment, I chose to believe that God wanted to do something good for me. I felt how small my faith actually was. I prayed as did the apostles, "Increase our faith" (Luke 17:5).

Charles Stanley says, "Whenever you see the word *believe* in the New Testament, you automatically know that it is a word of action."[4] What was I to do? In the midst of my spiritual anguish, I got the idea to read the Psalms aloud, kneeling. I had more confidence in the prayers of the Bible, and most of the Psalms were prayers. As David Jeremiah says in his book *When Your Worlds Fall Apart: See Past the Pain of the Present*:

> The psalms bear witness to the fact that we aren't the first to walk down the difficult roads of disappointment and persecution and bitterness. Here we find hope in the time of storm, even when the thunder and lightning cause us to run for shelter. As we read the Book of Psalms, we feel as if our story has been recorded before we have lived it. And if the problems have been there before us, the solutions must be there for us too. There can be no more powerful healing balm than the wisdom we find in this book, positioned strategically in the center of the Bible.[5]

I turned to the Lord and found forgiveness to make a new start. I understood that discouragement did not come from God. As I read the Psalms, crying out to God for help, my spiritual condition improved.

"Your word is a lamp to my feet and a light unto my path" (Psalm 119:105). And what a lamp God's Word was to me!

If you ever get to the same point as I did, you need Scripture as I did. In his book *Disappointment with God*, Philip Yancey posits:

---

3   Dallas Villard, *The Divine Conspiracy: Rediscovering Our Hidden Life in God* (San Francisco, CA: HarperOne, 1999), p. 237.

4   Charles F. Stanley, *In Step With God: Understanding* (Nashville, TN: Thomas Nelson, 2008), p. 175.

5   David Jeremiah, *When Your World Falls Apart: See Past the Pain of the Present* (Nashville, TN: Thomas Nelson, 2000), p. 226.

Alone for Christ

> God wanted faith, the Bible says, and that is the lesson Abraham finally learned. He learned to believe when there was no reason left to believe.... Somehow, that 'faith' was what God valued and it soon became clear that faith was the best way for humans to express a love for God.[6]

My hopes began to grow in my soul like a small green shoot on a plant. I asked for a sign from God that things would change: I opened the Bible with my eyes closed.

I had a degree in theology and yet I acted like a beginner in faith, opening the Bible at random. It is good that God walks alongside us, taking our steps with us.

I opened my eyes and read Isaiah 60. I was drawn to a few verses: "Then you will look and be radiant, your heart will throb and swell with joy; the wealth on the seas will be brought to you, to you the riches of the nations will come" (verse 5).

"Your gates will always stand open, they will never be shut, day or night, so that men may bring you the wealth of the nations" (verse 11).

"Instead of bronze I will bring you gold and silver in place of iron. Instead of wood, I will bring you bronze, and iron in place of stones. I will make peace your governor and righteousness your ruler" (verse 17).

The chapter ends with these words: "I am the Lord; in its time I will do this swiftly" (verse 22).

I read this chapter on my knees and then stood up in disbelief almost as did Abraham's wife, Sarah. I said, "Who am I that God should give me the wealth of the nations?" But a thought came to my mind: *You are looking in the wrong direction. Do not look at yourself but at the Lord. He is going to do that not because of what you are, but because of who He is.*

I knelt back and thanked God for these treasures of promises. Each of His promises stirs up our faith. I began to think that God would bless me in a financial way.

---

6   Philip Yancey, *Disappointment With God: Three Questions No One Asks Aloud* (Grand Rapids, MI: Zondervan, 1988), pp. 71, 72.

At the end of every year, we used to draw a card with a Bible promise from a basket in our church. I picked one and read the following on the back of it: "The Lord will send a blessing on your barns and on everything you put your hand to. The Lord your God will bless you in the land he is giving you" (Deut 28:8).

I figure out that God was going to move us to another country. Where? I did not know yet, but I believed it was only a matter of time. I was not afraid to go into the unknown because I felt a deep longing to have fresh experiences with God. I had not had any challenges for a long time, and ongoing routines diminished my faith.

We brought the issue of immigration before God. We wanted to distinguish foolishness from faith. We waited for His answer for few years. "In some ways, 'waiting on the Lord' is the hardest part of trusting. It is not the same as 'waiting around.' It is putting yourself with utter vulnerability in his hands."[7]

In the meantime, we experienced unspeakable joy when our son made a decision for baptism; he was sixteen years old. His baptism was like a triumphal arch for our family. Emanuel said, "I was baptized twice: once in my mother's womb and now a second time."

I exclaimed, "Here at last, a member of my family, the most important one, entered the water of baptism."

One day a family from church told us they had applied for immigration to Canada and suggested for us to do the same. At first I did not want to hear about it. Canada? It was too far away.

But then I gave it a second thought: *what if this is God's will?* We began to pray for Canada. When I completed the assessment on the Internet, I found that we did not meet the score because we were no longer young. In addition, we found out that the interviewer was very demanding.

If this was God's will, however, He would make us succeed. When we passed the interview, we realized, in hindsight, why Emanuel had to attend a high school that taught in English; he had to end up in Canada.

---

7   John Ortberg, *If You Want to Walk on Water, You've Got to Get Out of the Boat* (Grand Rapids, MI: Zondervan, 2001), p. 25.

Next, we needed money for immigration. We put the car up for sale and found a buyer quite quickly. We put the house built near the forest up for sale also. We arrived at an understanding as to why it was providential that we built that house. However, we waited for a long time until we finally received a call from a real estate agent who wanted to purchase the house for himself. The amount he offered us was more than we hoped to receive.

We went to a public notary to do up the purchase agreement and came across a seemingly insurmountable obstacle. We owned the title to the property, but we needed a court order confirming that the land was inherited from Gabriel's grandparents.

My father-in-law's brothers had not yet gone to court to officially register the division of the inherited land. We left the public notary quite disconcerted.

The buyer proposed for us to go to another public notary, where our request was refused the same. We realized there was nothing we could do and went back home. After driving a few miles, our cell phone rang. It was our buyer calling to tell us: "Come back! I still know of another public notary. It is in another city, but it is worth a try."

Hoping against hope, we went. The public notary looked at our documents and approved the draft of the sale. It was dark outside by the time we left with the money, but light flooded our souls. Dale Bruner wrote, "In accordance with the Scriptures, the end of human possibilities is often a meeting place with God."[8]

The family who encouraged us to immigrate to Canada had by this point already arrived in Canada. They told us they got their visas on their passports in four days. We hurried our preparations so that we could leave before the season when airfares were more expensive. We purchased our tickets even before we officially had visas on our passports.

There were few more days of school left, and I went to see the principal to ask him to facilitate the closing of my son's final marks. It was Thursday, and to be more convincing, I took the airline tickets to show him that the departure was scheduled for the following Tuesday.

---

8   Frederick Dale Bruner, *Matthew: A Commentary; The Churchbook: Matthew 13–28* (Dallas, TX: Word Inc., 1985), Vol. 2, p. 533.

The principal agreed and told me to come the following day to get my son's paper. When I got home, I received a call from the high school secretary asking me to come back to get my airline ticket. One of the student's parents found it at the bus stop and thought it must belong to someone from the school. I was shocked; I had never lost a penny in my life. What would we have done without one of the air tickets?

That very same Thursday, we went to say goodbye to our colleagues from the union at a farewell lunch. (We have worked at the union for fourteen years.) After the lunch I went to the embassy to pick up the passports; four business days had passed, and I was hoping that our visas would take no longer than they did in the other family's experience. You can imagine how I felt when the clerk told me it would take twenty-one business days. That meant we had to wait over a month. *What should we do? Go forward in faith!*

Monday we packed everything in our suitcases. Then we went to the embassy once again; this time my husband went to the teller. While I waited outside, I heard my name called. I went to the teller, who proceeded to argue with me because she had already told me when I was to come back; she was upset I had come back so soon. I apologized and told her that our airline tickets were for the next day. She said, "Show me the air tickets."

I had the flight tickets with me. She took them and went to the consul. It was near the end of the hours of operation, but they stayed overtime to draw our landing papers. What the family who had just arrived in Canada didn't know was that the landing papers lasted twenty-one days and the visa only four days. The embassy clerk wished us a good journey!

Chapter 9

In the New World

Once in Canada, we were delighted by the wonderful landscape, organized system, and good-mannered people. I want to emphasize once again the importance of the church. If you are part of a church, wherever you go in the world, you will have friends and not feel alone.

We felt accommodated in the new world thanks to the support of church brethren. My husband started to work with an Adventist; my son continued his high school education, and I started to take courses. Being in a foreign country, I realized it was imperative to know how the finance system worked.

I asked God to guide me to the job He wanted me to do and to be accepted at the very first interview. I started working in insurance, but I am not gifted in sales, I am not talkative, and I do not like to persuade clients. As a sales person, you have to relate easily with the people, and this was not my type of position. In fact, I am the "office mouse" type that Teacher Loblaw mentioned, as you may recall. In addition, English was my second language. Nevertheless, I went forward in faith despite my inadequacy for the job.

After a brief training, I went to the clients. I prayed before meeting the first customer. God helped me and I sold an insurance policy. I had a few more sales that week, but I had no idea if it was enough.

Soon I had to attend my first meeting with all the agents, and I was late. When I reached the door, I stopped in my tracks, utterly ashamed to come in. I heard the president talking. At one point they started to applaud. I told to myself: *this is my time to sneak in through the door because they are less attentive at the moment.* I slowly and quietly opened the door, and the president suddenly pointed to me, saying, "Look, she is the one!" The agents started to clap even louder. The president continued, "And she does not have a car." To my surprise, I had the greatest production of the week. It was a success for a new agent. In addition, as the president said, I did not have a car.

On our arrival in Canada, we purchased a car for my husband to go to work. I did not get my driver's license yet. To go from one client to another by bus or subway took a lot of time. I needed a car, but I first had to pass the driver's exam.

I passed the theoretical test but failed the driving test. It was the first time in my life that I had failed a test. I felt bad, but I knew it was because of my lack of practice. Also, I took this as an opportunity to sympathize with other people who experienced failure.

My son, on the other hand, had gotten his driver's license one month earlier and already drove like Michael Schumacher, seven-times world champion Formula One driver. My son offered to train me in addition to the driving school trainer's lessons, and I passed the exam.

I purchased a small car to be able to park it easily. My son still accompanied me for one more week of driving. There were times when he drove from the passenger seat. I was scared when I drove alone; my knees trembled whenever I made a left turn at a traffic light. When I first entered the freeway, I took the first entrance and promptly took the very next exit.

However, when you surrender God and ask Him to help you, He does marvelous things. After a few months of driving, I was able to drive with one hand while eating with the other or doing something else. When traffic was slow, I made phone calls to customers. I would hold the wheel with one hand and write down the address of the client with the other one. Very soon my car was full of papers and looked like an office.

On another note, I would like to discourage driving with divided attention and will, therefore, relate what happened to me one winter day. It started to snow while I was driving downtown. The snow was soft and I was talking on the phone. I was paying attention to keep the tram's railway between the wheels to avoid slipping, but I wasn't Napoleon. At one point, one of the wheels got on the rail, and my car slipped on the horizontal line. Thank God there was no car behind me. I slowed down but could not stop the car, which was moving toward the sidewalk. It was my first time driving in snow, and I did not know how to brake properly. My car slid like a sleigh and went up the sidewalk ready to smash into the fence. I screamed, as women do, and I swerved left. I avoided hitting the fence but my car moved toward the roadside pole. I pulled the steering wheel a little bit and just missed the pole. Finally, my car came to a stop on the sidewalk. I thanked God for saving me from an accident. From then on, I no longer booked any appointments by phone while driving.

I agreed with my husband that a bigger car was heavier and more stable in winter than mine. I took his van. My husband purchased another car for himself, and we bought a car for our Schumacher. Now we had four cars for three drivers.

Sometimes I would not sell any policies for weeks in a row. In His wisdom, God allowed to undergo a "dry season" to remind me and make it clear where my success was coming from. I read the book *Escape to God* by Jim Hohnberger.[1] He wrote about how God helped him to be first in sales. God did this for me as well. While I drove to meet clients, I would sing Christian hymns and earnestly pray, "Heavenly Father, I am doing what I like to do and what is easy for me to do: to sing. Please do for me that which is difficult for me to do."

I had the opportunity to enter many houses, to meet people from all continents and understand some of their culture. I talked to "kings" because many of them held high positions in their countries.

However, anyone who works in sales knows the negatives of this job. Few agents withstand the stress and often give up within the first months. This is the kind of job where you have very little control. You do not know how the person in front of you will react. For example, you never knew at what emotional context or in what life situation you were finding that person. I realized God had led me to this job to teach me dependence on Him once again.

My prior work was pretty well the same from month to month. I knew the deadlines for payment of invoices, paychecks, and balance sheets. In insurance, however, one day did not look like the previous day. I assigned each sale to God's help. "The Lord will make you the head, not the tail. If you pay attention to the commands of the Lord your God that I give you this day and carefully follow them, you will always be at the top, never at the bottom" (Deut. 28:13).

---

1   Jim Hohnberger, *Escape to God: How Our Family Left the Rat Race Behind to Search for Genuine Spirituality and the Simple Life* (Nampa, ID: Pacific Press Publishing Association, 2001).

I felt a compelling desire to visit my country, so I did. We had already filed the immigration papers on behalf of Gabriel's parents. My mother was glad to hear this. For the first time since my conversion, my mom told me that I did something that pleased her. This was proof that the Holy Spirit was working on her heart, and her qualities came to the surface. Exactly one month later, my mom passed away. My dad had lived for another eleven years after my conversion, and my mother lived another eleven years after my dad's death.

Please pray for my sister and brother. I am convinced that these precious souls would make zealous workers for God if they turned to Him. My sister, with her innate generosity, would sacrifice much for the cause of God.

One day, God impressed me to quit my insurance job. I had enrolled in a course for a different vocation and passed the exam. Then I informed the president; he was shocked.

"No way. You achieved such amazing performance."

"Mr. President, I have made my decision."

"Wait a minute! We have to discuss this. I do not have time now, as I am going to a conference in the U.S. and will be back in two weeks. I have big plans for you, to send you for training in the States to become a manager."

I had to wait two weeks. This time I thought I would use the hamburger technique: I will start with a positive factor, then state the negative, and finish with another positive.

"Mr. President, thank you so much for your intention to promote me. I appreciate what you are willing to do for me—"

I could not continue because he started to talk. He thought I bit the bait and explained to me how he saw my future career. He was fully satisfied thinking that he had managed to make me change my mind about quitting. When he stopped talking, I said, "Thank you, but..." When I said "but," his facial expression changed.

"I have chosen to work in another field. I already took the exam," I finished.

Alone for Christ

I felt pity for him. I had not intended to give him false hopes, but he had jumped to the wrong conclusion. He once again did his best to make me change my mind.

"You have a successful career in insurance."

"I want to try something else."

"The field where you want to work is more difficult than this."

"I guess so, but I am a determined person."

"You made good money."

I said to myself, *God gave me this money as He promised.* I replied, "Money is not my god."

"You can always come back."

"Thank you, Mr. President."

I left without looking back. God had appointed for me the time to leave. I did not know at the time that the next month would bring a recession and a significant drop in sales. My commission would have suffered considerably had I stayed at my old job. I didn't know, but God knew. The company that hired me offered me a fixed salary, which is just what I needed during a recession. It is time that we listen carefully to God's whisper telling us what to do. Later, I graduated college and an accounting program at the university and started working as an accountant.

Gabriel and Marinela in church

God worked a new wonder in our lives: Gabriel's parents received approval for Canadian residence and came to live with us. Here is how the cycle is repeated: my mother-in-law who treated her in-laws lovingly, gained me, a daughter who loves her. The Bible teaches that we will reap what we sow and even more than we sow.

I would like to add something about Gabriel's mother. She wanted to read the entire Bible in a month and asked God to give her strength. She was sixty-nine years old when she read the Bible even thirteen times that year. She did not read it in a hurry, but loudly and carefully. At one point I was concerned that her vision would suffer. On the contrary, her vision improved; she started to read without reading glasses. She experienced the phenomenon that the more you read the Bible, the faster you can read it. This is the incredible power of God that comes to us through prayer. I like Ravi Zacharias' description of the Bible:

> God's Word is the best bridge between the old and the new, between the body and the soul, between the temporal and the eternal, between God and humanity. The inscription is old but the blessing is always new. The language is old but the application is new. The originals are old but the originality is new—the forward and the backward.[2]

I am so happy that my husband was called to be a pastor. Words cannot express my gratitude to God.

---

2   Ravi Zacharias, *Recapture the Wonder: Experiencing God's Amazing Promise of Childlike Joy* (Nashville, TN: Integrity Publishers, 2003), p. 146.

Gabriel and Marinela, as a pastoral family

Epilogue

Pastor John Ortberg wrote about what happened to him on a vacation at a ranch in Arizona:

> I rode out with five ranch hands to take the herd of horses to pasture about three miles away.... My horse was named Reverse, based on his particular eccentricity of going backward anytime someone was foolish enough to pull on his reins. I made a mental note not to do that.... One of the ranch hands decided to make a race of the return trip.... Reverse started to make his move. Instinctively, I pulled on the reins as hard as I could. Reverse rose up on his hind legs and took a few steps backward... and then took off like a bat out of... a cannon.... We were not sauntering or trotting—this was all-out sprinting as in a scene from a movie. The five ranch hands were college-age guys who lived on horseback all summer long, racing their horses as fast as they could. Reverse and I passed four of them. I say "Reverse and I," but the truth is he was doing most of the work. I was just waiting to die....
>
> While I was wondering how my wife would spend the life insurance policy, the strangest thing happened. I realized there was a good chance I would survive this, and then it became one of the most exhilarating moments I had all week....
>
> By the time we pulled up to the fence, I knew this had been the ride of my life. I would not have missed this experience for anything.... My only choice had been to say

yes or no to the ride. I had to decide whether I had enough faith to ride the horse. When I mounted that horse, I did not have a clue as to what was going to happen to me…. Once I took a single step, once I got into the saddle, a whole world of experience was set in motion. Everything else was up to the horse.[1]

I could say as did Pastor Ortberg: *this was the race of my life.* God sustained me with His grace and love along my path. I can easily fall into discouragement due to my temperament. I do not carry the "risky" gene, as researchers call people who like adventure. If God would not strengthen me, I could not go against the tide. My story is the story of a war between faith and fear; despite my fears, I chose to say yes to God.

I did not have a clue as to what was going to happen to me. But once I took my first step of faith, a whole world of experiences opened to me. All that followed depended only on God.

Many people like to hear stories about how powerful our God is, but pure information is not enough. You have to take your own first step of faith. "There will come a time when God will require you to do the same— launch out and leave your comfort zone for a place where you must trust Him and not on your ability to get the job done. You won't be able to touch the bottom of the lake or the pool. No human line of security will be available. There will be only one line of hope, and that is the one tied to Him—and it is all you need."[2]

Your quest to know the Lord leads you to a deeper level—one that changes your life focus forever. " 'I tell you the truth,' Jesus replied, 'no one who has left home or brothers or sisters or mother or father or children or fields for me and the gospel will fall to receive a hundred times as much in this present age (homes, brothers, sisters, mothers, children and fields—and with them, persecutions) and in the age to come, eternal life' " (Mark 10:29, 30). I am living proof of this promise. We believers can expect persecution from the world and even our own family. Nobody ever said the Christian walk was easy. But is there anything in the world that is of greater importance? Remember that those willing to endure hardship will in time receive manifold blessings.

---

1 John Ortberg, *If You Want to Walk on Water, You've Got to Get Out of the Boat* (Grand Rapids, MI: Zondervan, 2001), pp. 75–77.

2 Charles F. Stanley, *In Step With God: Understanding* (Nashville, TN: Thomas Nelson, 2008), p. 215.

I would like to quote John Newton, author of the lyrics to "Amazing Grace":

"I am not what I ought to be,

I am not what I want to be,

I am not what I hope to be in another world;

But still I am not what I once used to be,

And by the grace of God I am what I am."

I praise God because He called me to Him and helped me in all my trials. When you get on track with God's plan and begin to understand all that it entails, you will find life in all its fullness. You will see that being on a God-guided adventure is truly living life with an eternal hope.

We invite you to view the complete
selection of titles we publish at:

www.TEACHServices.com

Please write or email us your praises, reactions,
or thoughts about this or any other book we publish at:

TEACH Services, Inc.
P U B L I S H I N G
www.TEACHServices.com

info@TEACHServices.com

TEACH Services, Inc., titles may be purchased in bulk for
educational, business, fund-raising, or sales promotional use.
For information, please e-mail:

BulkSales@TEACHServices.com

Finally, if you are interested in seeing
your own book in print, please contact us at

publishing@TEACHServices.com

We would be happy to review your manuscript for free.

www.ingramcontent.com/pod-product-compliance
Lightning Source LLC
Chambersburg PA
CBHW060544100426
42742CB00013B/2446